Ratner-Sec.Reg.—1

SECURITIES REGULATION
IN A NUTSHELL

by

DAVID L. RATNER

Professor of Law
Cornell University

ST. PAUL, MINN.
WEST PUBLISHING CO.
1978

Library of Congress Catalog Card Number: 77–92720

Ratner—Sec.Reg.

PREFACE

This book is designed for lawyers, law students and others who are seeking an understanding of the basic content and organization of federal (and state) securities law.

The growth and elaboration of federal securities law in recent years has been phenomenal. In this "nutshell," I have tried to summarize the essential background and current status of each major area, while keeping details and citations to a minimum. I have, of course, included references to the relevant statutes, SEC rules and releases, and other governmental materials, as well as to "leading cases," where they exist, and to illustrative cases in other areas. I have not cited any secondary materials; there are simply too many of them.

This book will not answer all of your questions about securities law. It should, however, answer most of your basic ones and help you to find the answers to the others. I enjoyed putting this book together; I hope you will find it useful and informative.

DAVID L. RATNER

Ithaca, New York
October, 1977

*

OUTLINE

I. INTRODUCTION

II. REGULATION OF PUBLIC OFFERINGS

III. REGULATION OF PUBLICLY–HELD COMPANIES

IV. ANTIFRAUD PROVISIONS

V. REGULATION OF THE SECURITIES BUSINESS

VI. REGULATION OF INVESTMENT COMPANIES

VII. SANCTIONS FOR VIOLATIONS

VIII. CIVIL LIABILITIES

IX. EXTRATERRITORIAL APPLICATION

X. STATE REGULATION

OUTLINE

TABLE OF CASES

References are to Pages

TABLE OF CASES

TABLE OF CASES

TABLE OF CASES

TABLE OF CASES

TABLE OF CASES

TABLE OF CASES

TABLE OF CASES

TABLE OF CASES

*

TABLE OF STATUTES AND RULES

SECURITIES ACT OF 1933

(15 USC § 77)

TABLE OF STATUTES AND RULES

1933 ACT RULES
(17 CFR § 230.–)

SECURITIES EXCHANGE ACT OF 1934
(15 USC § 78)

TABLE OF STATUTES AND RULES

TABLE OF STATUTES AND RULES

1934 ACT RULES

(17 CFR § 240.–)

INVESTMENT COMPANY ACT OF 1940

15 USC § 80a

TABLE OF STATUTES AND RULES

INVESTMENT ADVISERS ACT OF 1940

15 USC § 80b

SECURITIES INVESTOR PROTECTION ACT OF 1970

15 USC § 78aaa et seq.

UNIFORM SECURITIES ACT

7 Unif.Laws Ann. 691 (1970)

ABBREVIATIONS

CCH —Commerce Clearing House Federal Securities Law Reports
FRB —Federal Reserve Board
IAA —Investment Advisers Act of 1940
ICA —Investment Company Act of 1940
NASD—National Association of Securities Dealers
NYSE—New York Stock Exchange
OTC —Over-the-counter (market)
Rel. —(SEC) Release
RRI —(SEC) Rules Relating to Investigations
SA —Securities Act of 1933
SEA —Securities Exchange Act of 1934
SEC —Securities and Exchange Commission
SIPA —Securities Investor Protection Act of 1970
SIPC —Securities Investor Protection Corporation
SRO —Self-regulatory organization
USA —Uniform Securities Act

†

SECURITIES REGULATION

I. INTRODUCTION

Securities differ from most other commodities in which people deal. They have no intrinsic value in themselves—they represent rights in something else. The value of a bond, note or other promise to pay depends on the financial condition of the promisor. The value of a share of stock depends on the profitability or future prospects of the corporation or other entity which issued it; its market price depends on how much other people are willing to pay for it, based on their evaluation of those prospects.

The distinctive features of securities give a distinctive coloration to regulation of transactions in securities, in contrast to the regulation of transactions in other types of goods. Most goods are produced, distributed and used or consumed; governmental regulation focuses on protecting the ultimate consumer against dangerous articles, misleading advertising, and unfair or non-competitive pricing practices. Securities are different.

First, securities are created, rather than produced. They can be issued in unlimited amounts, virtually without cost, since they are nothing in themselves but represent only an interest in something else. An important focus of securities laws, therefore, is assuring that, when securities are created and offered to the public, investors have an accurate idea of what that "something else" is and how much of an interest in it the particular security represents.

Second, securities are not used or consumed by their purchasers. They become a kind of currency, traded in the so-called "secondary markets" at fluctuating prices. These "secondary" transactions far outweigh, in number and volume, the offerings of newly-created securities. A second important focus of securities law, therefore, is to assure that there is a continuous flow of information about the corporation or other entity whose securities are being traded, with additional disclosure whenever security holders are being asked to vote, or make some other decision, with respect to the securities they hold.

Third, because the trading markets for securities are uniquely susceptible to manipulative and deceptive practices, all securities laws contain general "antifraud" provisions. These have been interpreted to apply not only to manipulation of securities prices, but also to trading by "insiders" on the basis of non-public information and to various kinds of misstatements by corporate management and others.

Fourth, since a large industry has grown up to buy and sell securities for investors and traders, securities laws are concerned with the regulation of people and firms engaged in that business, to assure that they do not take advantage of their superior experience and access to overreach their non-professional customers.

Finally, securities laws provide for a variety of governmental sanctions against those who violate their prohibitions, as well as civil liability to persons injured by such violations. In addition, the courts have implied the existence of civil liabilities in situations where they are not expressly provided by statute.

§ 1. The Securities Markets

The facilities through which securities are traded are known as "markets". These markets may have physical locations, but in many cases are simply formal or informal systems of communication through which buyers and sellers make their interests known and consummate transactions.

In terms of dollar volume, the largest securities market is the bond market—trading in the debt instruments issued by the United States government, by state and local governments, and by corporations. However, since the bond market attracts more interest from professional and institutional investors than from the general public, and since federal, state and local government obligations are exempt from most of the direct regulatory provisions of the federal securities laws, the bond markets have in recent years occupied only a small part of the attention of securities regulators.

The principal focus of securities regulation is on the markets for common stocks. There are two types of stock markets now operating in the United States—"exchange" markets and "over-the-counter" markets. An "exchange" market, of which the New York Stock Exchange (NYSE) is by far the largest, operates in a physical facility with a trading "floor" to which all transactions in a particular security are supposed to be directed. The NYSE (and, to a lesser extent, the other exchanges) has traditionally operated in a very rigid manner, prescribing the number and qualifications of members, the functions each member may perform, and (until 1975) the commission rate to be charged on all transactions. The over-the-counter (OTC) market, on the other hand, has traditionally been completely unstructured, without any physical facility, and with any qualified firm being free to engage in any types of activities with respect to any securities.

As far as the individual buyer or seller of stocks is concerned, the significant difference between an exchange and OTC transaction is the function performed by the firm with which he deals. In the case of an exchange transaction, his firm acts as a "broker"—that it, as an agent for the customer's account—and charges him a commission for its services. The only person permitted to act as a "dealer" or "make a market" in the stock on the exchange floor (that is, to buy and sell the security for his own account) is the registered "specialist" in that stock. The broker transmits the customer's order to the exchange floor where it is generally executed by buying from or selling to either the specialist or another customer whose broker has left his order on the specialist's "book."

In the OTC market, on the other hand, there is no exchange floor, only a computer and telephone communication network. Any number of firms may act as "dealers" or "market makers" in a particular stock and may deal directly with public customers in that stock. If the firm through which a customer orders a particular stock is not a dealer in that stock, it will normally purchase it for him as broker from one of the dealers making a market in that stock. In many cases, however, the firm will solicit orders from customers in stocks in which it is making a market, selling the stock to the customer as principal at a mark-up over the price it is currently quoting to brokers. Since retail firms commonly act simultaneously as brokers in exchange-listed stocks and as dealers in OTC stocks, this may cause some confusion on the part of customers.

A firm selling stock to a customer as part of an underwritten offering of a new issue (whether of a listed or OTC stock) normally sells to the customer as principal at a fixed price (equal to or slightly below the current market price, in the case of a security which is already publicly traded). The dealer's compensation in that case comes out of the "spread" between the public offering price and the net proceeds paid to the issuer (or other person on whose behalf the distribution is being made).

Over the past two decades, two factors have substantially blurred the distinctions between exchange and OTC markets. The first is modern computer and communication technology, which has revolutionized the operation of the over-the-counter market, and has raised serious questions about the necessity and desirability of a physical exchange "floor." At the same time, trading in common stocks, particularly those listed on the New York Stock Exchange, has been increasingly dominated by "institutional investors"—principally pension funds, mutual funds, bank trust departments, and insurance companies—with individual investors accounting for a continually decreasing percentage of trading volume. The distinctive trading practices of institutions, and the types of services they require and do not require, have put serious strains on the traditional market mechanisms. Current efforts within the industry and the government are focused on rationalizing the market structure and determining who can do business and on what terms in the developing "national market system".

(a) The Securities Industry

The securities industry is characterized by great diversity, both in size and function. There are probably about 5,000 firms engaged in one or more types of securities activities, ranging from large firms engaged in brokerage, market-making, underwriting, investment advice and fund management, as well as commodities, real estate dealings and a variety of other financial service activities, down to one-man firms engaged solely in selling mutual fund shares or dealing in a few securities of solely local interest.

There has always been a substantial failure rate among small securities firms, which commence operations during periods of high trading volume and fold when volume declines. In 1969 and 1970, however, as a result of operational breakdowns, unsound capital structures, and rapidly declining volume and prices for securities, there was an unprecedented series of failures of large NYSE member firms, almost causing the collapse of the industry. This near-collapse triggered a number of governmental studies, culminating in the imposition of new financial responsibility requirements on securities firms. It also led to efforts, which are still continuing, to devise a more rational and efficient system for the clearing and settlement of securities transactions.

Since the passage in 1933 of the Glass-Steagall Act, prohibiting banks from dealing in securities (except government bonds), the securities business has consisted of a relatively separate and well-defined group of firms. However, with the increasing tendency for individuals to make their equity investments indirectly through institutions, rather than trading directly in stock for their own account, securities firms have come increasingly into competition with banks and insurance companies, particularly with respect to the management of pension funds. This competition has placed severe strains on the existing regulatory structure, under which securities firms, banks and insurance companies are regulated by different agencies with entirely different concerns and approaches.

§ 2. State and Federal Securities Laws

Securities transactions are subject to regulation under both federal and state law. Since the federal securities laws are based on Congress' power to regulate interstate commerce, they generally apply only to transactions involving "the use of any means or instruments of transportation or communication in interstate commerce or of the mails." The courts have been willing to find the requisite use of interstate commerce facilities in doubtful situations. Use of the mails to accomplish any part of the transaction, including payment or confirmation after a sale, is sufficient to support federal jurisdiction. An in*tra*state telephone call has also been held to involve the use of in*ter*state facilities.

Federal securities laws specifically preserve the right of the states to regulate securities transactions, so that the states remain free to supplement or duplicate federal requirements to whatever extent they choose.

State securities laws, commonly known as "blue sky" laws, generally provide for registration of broker-dealers, registration of securities to be offered or traded in the state, and sanctions against fraudulent activities. A Uniform Securities Act (USA), promulgated in 1956, has been substantially or partially adopted in more than 30 states, but state securities law is still characterized by great diversity of language and interpretation.

Federal securities law basically consists of six statutes enacted between 1933 and 1940, and periodically amended in the intervening years, and one statute enacted in 1970. The statutes are:

Securities Act of 1933 (SA)

Securities Exchange Act of 1934 (SEA)

Public Utility Holding Company Act of 1935 (PUHCA)

Trust Indenture Act of 1939 (TIA)

Investment Company Act of 1940 (ICA)

Investment Advisers Act of 1940 (IAA)

Securities Investor Protection Act of 1970 (SIPA)

The *Securities Act of 1933* regulates public offerings of securities. It prohibits offers and sales of securities which are not registered with the Securities and Exchange Commission (SEC), subject to exemptions for enumerated kinds of securities and transactions. It also prohibits fraudulent or deceptive practices in any offer or sale of securities.

The *Securities Exchange Act of 1934* extended federal regulation to trading in securities which are already issued and outstanding. Unlike the 1933 Act, which focuses on a single regulatory provision, the 1934 Act contains a number of distinct groups of provisions, aimed at different participants in the securities trading process. The Act established the Securities and Exchange Commission and transferred to it the responsibility for administration of the 1933 Act (which had originally been assigned to the Federal Trade Commission). Other provisions of the Act impose disclosure and other requirements on publicly-held corporations; prohibit various "manipulative or deceptive devices or contrivances" in connection with the purchase or sale of securities; restrict the amount of credit that may be extended for the purchase of securities; require brokers and dealers to register with the SEC and regulate their activities; and provide for SEC registration and supervision of national securities exchanges and associations, clearing agencies, transfer agents, and securities information processors. As a result of Congressional inquiries into an operational and financial crisis which engulfed the securities industry in the period from 1968 to 1970, the Securities Exchange Act was substantially amended in 1975 to increase the SEC's authority over national securities exchanges and the structure of the market system.

The *Public Utility Holding Company Act of 1935* was enacted to correct abuses which Congressional inquiries had disclosed in the financing and operation of electric and gas public utility holding company systems, and to achieve physical integration and corporate simplification of those systems. The SEC's functions under this Act were substantially completed by the 1950's, and it currently accounts for a very small part of the Commission's work.

The *Trust Indenture Act of 1939* applies generally to public issues of debt securities in excess of $1,000,000. Even though the issue is registered under the 1933 Act, the indenture covering the securities must also be qualified under the 1939 Act, which imposes standards of independence and responsibility on the indenture trustee and requires other provisions to be included in the indenture for the protection of the security holders.

The *Investment Company Act of 1940* gives the SEC regulatory authority over publicly-owned companies which are engaged primarily in the business of investing and trading in securities. The Act regulates the composition of the management of investment companies, their capital structure, approval of their advisory contracts and changes in investment policy, and requires SEC approval for any transactions by such companies with directors, officers or affiliates. It was amended in 1970 to impose additional controls on management compensation and sales charges.

The *Investment Advisers Act of 1940,* as amended in 1960, established a scheme of registration and regulation of investment advisers comparable to that contained in the 1934 Act with respect to broker-dealers.

The *Securities Investor Protection Act of 1970* established the Securities Investor Protection Corporation (SIPC), which has power to supervise the liquidation of securities firms which get into financial difficulties, and to arrange for the payment of claims asserted by their customers.

The American Law Institute is currently engaged in drafting a "Federal Securities Code", designed to replace the seven laws described above. The proposed Code would not make any major substantive changes in the law, but is designed to deal with certain "problems" under existing law, including (a) the "complications" arising from inconsistent definitions, as well as procedural and jurisdictional provisions, in the different acts, (b) the overemphasis in the disclosure provisions on "public offerings" rather than periodic reporting requirements, and (c) the "chaotic" development of civil liabilities resulting from "broad judicial implication of private rights of action" under various provisions of existing law. The Institute is expected to give final approval to the proposed Code in May 1978, after which it will be submitted to Congress for consideration.

§ 3. The Securities and Exchange Commission

The Securities and Exchange Commission (SEC) is the agency charged with principal responsibility for the enforcement and administration of the federal securities laws. The 1934 Act provides that the SEC shall consist of five members appointed by the President for five-year terms (the term of one Commissioner expires each year), not more than three of whom shall be members of the same political party.

Among lawyers, and among students of governmental process, the SEC generally enjoys a high reputation. It has been noteworthy for the level of intelligence and integrity of its staff, the flexibility and informality of many of its procedures, and its avoidance of the political and economic pitfalls in which many other regulatory agencies have found themselves trapped. Its disclosure and enforcement policies have also been credited with making an important contribution to the generally favorable reputation which American corporate securities and American securities markets enjoy, not only among American investors, but also in foreign countries.

The SEC Staff. While the Commission itself is ultimately responsible for all decisions, the day-to-day administration of the Acts is largely delegated to the staff. In terms of SEC "programs", the Commission has estimated that about 34% of its staff is engaged in "fraud prevention", 27% in "disclosure", 25% in regulation of broker-dealers and the markets, 13% in regulation of investment companies and investment advisers, and 2% in public utility holding company regulation. About two-thirds of the staff is located at the Commission's head office in Washington, and the remainder in 9 regional and 8 branch offices in financial centers around the country. The SEC has a very small economic staff, and engages in almost none of the rate-setting and franchise-granting activities which occupy a large part of the attention of most other regulatory agencies.

"Self-Regulation". Rather than relying solely on regulation by the SEC, the federal securities laws reserve a uniquely important role for "self-regulation" by industry and professional groups. Stock exchanges had been regulating the activities of their members for more than 140 years prior to the passage of the Securities Exchange Act of 1934, and that Act incorporated the exchanges into the regulatory structure, subject to certain oversight powers in the SEC. When Congress decided to impose more comprehensive regulation on over-the-counter securities dealers in 1938, and on municipal securities dealers in 1975, it adopted a similar approach, authorizing the establishment of the National Association of Securities Dealers (NASD) and the Municipal Securities Rulemaking Board (MSRB) as self-regulatory organizations for those respective groups.

§ 4. Sources of Securities Law

The starting point in analyzing any question of federal securities law is of course the statutes. The statutes are, however, quite sketchy or ambiguous in many important areas, so that it is necessary to resort to supplemental sources of law. These are of two kinds: rules and other statements of general applicability issued by the SEC (or self-regulatory organizations), and reports of decided cases.

The SEC has broad rule-making powers under the various statutes it administers, and has exercised its authority by prescribing at least three different kinds of rules. The first category consists of procedural and technical rules (e. g., rules prescribing numbers of copies to be filed); the second category consists of definitions of terms used in the law (e. g., SA Rule 146, defining what constitutes a "public offering"); the third category consists of substantive rules adopted pursuant to a Congressional delegation of authority (e. g., the proxy solicitation rules under SEA § 14).

Supplementing the SEC's rules are its forms for the various statements and reports which issuers, broker-dealers and others are required to file under the Acts. Since disclosure is such an important part of the regulatory pattern, these forms (which have the legal force of rules) play an important part in defining the extent of the disclosure obligation.

Beyond the rules and forms, the SEC goes in for a good deal of "informal law-making", setting forth the views of the Commission or its staff on questions of current concern, without stating them in the form of legal requirements. The principal media for these statements are SEC "Releases" which, as the name implies, are simply statements distributed to the press, to companies and firms registered with the Commission, and to other interested persons.

In addition to general public statements of policy, the staff has, since the Commission's early days, been willing to respond to individual private inquiries as to whether a certain transaction could be carried out in a specified manner. These responses are known as "no-action" letters, because they customarily state that "the staff will recommend no action to the Commission" if the transaction is done in the specified manner.

In some areas of federal securities law, notably in the registration provisions of the 1933 Act, most of the "law" is found in the rules, forms, and policy statements of the Commission, and very little in the form of decided "cases". In other areas, however, notably under the general anti-fraud provisions of the 1934 Act, there is very little in the way of formal rules, and the law has developed in the traditional "common law" manner, with courts and other tribunals deciding each case of the basis of precedents.

Decisions may be rendered in several different types of proceedings. The SEC itself may proceed in a number of ways if it discovers what it believes to be a violation of the law.

If the alleged violator is a broker-dealer or investment adviser required to register with it, the Commission can bring a proceeding to revoke or suspend the firm's registration or take other disciplinary action. If the alleged violator is an issuer seeking to sell securities under a 1933 Act registration statement, the Commission can bring a proceeding to suspend the effectiveness of the statement. In either case, the Commission staff acts as "prosecutor" and the Commission itself makes the final decision (after initial findings by an administrative law judge).

If the alleged violator is an issuer not currently making a registered public offering, or a person not registered with the Commission at all, then the Commission must go to court to obtain relief. The most common type of Commission proceeding is an application to a federal district court for an injunction against future violations. In a particularly egregious case, however, the Commission may refer the matter to the Department of Justice for prosecution as a criminal violation of the securities laws.

A person who believes himself to have been injured by a violation of the securities laws can bring a civil action in the courts for damages. He may sue either under the specific civil liability provisions of those laws, or assert an "implied" right of action under a provision prohibiting the activity in question. Beginning in the 1960's there was an enormous expansion in the number of private damage actions under the federal securities laws, particularly those asserting an implied right of action under the general antifraud provisions. However, since 1975, the Supreme Court has taken a much more restrictive view of the availability of these implied rights of action.

§ 5. Where to Find the Law

The most comprehensive and convenient source for all of the federal securities laws, SEC rules, forms, interpretations and decisions, and court decisions on securities matters is the loose-leaf Federal Securities Law Reporter published by Commerce Clearing House (CCH). This service is kept up to date with weekly supplements, and decisions and interpretations going back to 1941 can be found in annual or bi-annual "transfer binders". Pamphlet copies of the 1933 and 1934 Acts, and of the rules and forms governing the preparation of disclosure documents under those two acts, are also available from many financial printers who specialize in the preparation of such documents.

The official version of the federal securities laws is of course found in the United States Code (and in the United States Code Annotated) as §§ 77–80 of Title 15. Unfortunately, whoever was in charge of numbering the Code decided that the sections of the 1933 Act (15 U.S.C. § 77) should be numbered §§ 77a, 77b, 77c, etc. Thus § 5(b)(1) of the Act becomes 15 U.S.C. § 77e(b)(1), and § 12(2) become § 77m(2). The 1934 Act is handled in similar fashion in 15 U.S.C. § 78. Since everyone connected with securities regulation uses the section numbers of the Acts, rather than the Code references, the latter are omitted in this book.

The official version of the SEC rules can be found in volume 17 of the Code of Federal Regulations. Here the numbering system is more rational. 1933 Act rules are found in 17 C.F.R. § 230 under the rule number, and 1934 Act rules can be found in 17 C.F.R. § 240 in the same manner. Thus SA Rule 144 is 17 C.F.R. § 230.144, and SEA Rule 10b–5 is 17 C.F.R. § 240.10b–5.

SEC releases announcing the proposal or adoption of new rules, as well as those containing significant interpretations of the law, can be found in the Federal Register for the day on which the release was issued. Prior to 1973, however, other releases were not systematically or officially published in any form other than the mimeographed releases actually distributed by the Commission, and were simply numbered serially by reference to the Act or Acts to which they related, such as Securities Act Release No. 4434. From time to time, however, the SEC did publish compilations of "significant" releases under certain of the Acts. Since February 1973, the full text of all releases under all of the Acts is printed in a weekly publication called "SEC Docket", available through the Government Printing Office.

The SEC's "no-action" letters are now publicly available although not systematically published. They can be examined at the SEC office in Washington, and selected letters are published or summarized in the CCH Federal Securities Law Reporter of the BNA Securities Regulation and Law Reports.

The official texts of SEC decisions in administrative proceedings brought before it are distributed as "releases" at the time they are handed down, and are eventually printed and compiled in bound volumes of "SEC Decisions and Reports" (S.E.C.). This series currently covers decisions through June 1972.

Court decisions involving the federal securities laws are generally reported in full text in the CCH Federal Securities Law Reporter. Decisions of the Courts of Appeals, of course, also appear in West's Federal Reporter, Second Series (F.2d), and the more significant District Court decisions appear in the Federal Supplement (F.Supp.)

Confirmation of the maturing of "Securities Regulation" as a field of law came in 1972, when the West Digest System established it as a separate subject matter and reclassified under the new heading all of the cases which had previously lurked in scattered key numbers under "Licenses" and other headings. The Eighth Decennial Digest, therefore, contains a compilation of all federal and state securities cases reported in the National Reporter System up to 1976.

Up-to-date compilations of the constitutions, rules, and interpretations of the major stock exchanges and the NASD can be found in the loose-leaf stock exchange "Guides" and the "NASD Manual" published by CCH.

As far as state securities law is concerned, the most current and comprehensive compilation of statutes, rules and administrative and court decisions is the CCH Blue Sky Law Reporter, which contains separate sections covering the law of each of the 50 states. The securities law of any particular state can also be obtained through its published statutes, published administrative regulations (if any), and official and unofficial reports of its court decisions.

§ 6. The Definition of "Security"

The term "security" is defined in § 2(1) of the federal Securities Act of 1933 to include "any note, stock, treasury stock, bond, debenture, evidence of indebtedness, certificate of interest or participation in any profit-sharing agreement, collateral-trust certificate, preorganization certificate or subscription, transferable share, investment contract, voting-trust certificate, certificate of deposit for a security, fractional undivided interest in oil, gas, or other mineral rights, or, in general, any interest or instrument commonly known as a 'security', or any certificate of interest or participation in, temporary or interim certificate for, receipt for, guarantee of, or warrant or right to subscribe to or purchase, any of the foregoing." Substantially identical definitions are found in the other federal securities laws, see SEA § 3(a)(10), ICA § 2(a)(36), and in most state securities laws, see USA § 401(e).

Interpretive questions under these provisions have generally involved three different types of instruments: (a) instruments technically denominated "stock" or "notes," but issued for non-investment purposes, (b) special types of investment instruments issued by financial institutions, such as insurance companies and savings and loan associations, and (c) instruments evidencing investments in profit-seeking undertakings, which are not in the form of stock, notes or other traditional "securities."

(a) Stock and Notes

A share of stock will almost always be deemed to be a "security." However, in United Housing Foundation v. Forman, 421 U.S. 837 (1975), the Supreme Court held that shares of stock in a cooperative housing corporation were not "securities" under federal law where "the inducement to purchase was solely to acquire low-cost living space; it was not to invest for profit." The court rejected the "suggestion that the present transaction * * * must be considered a security transaction simply because the statutory definition of a security includes the words 'any * * * stock'" and reemphasized the "basic principle that has guided all of the Court's decisions in this area," that "form should be disregarded for substance and the emphasis should be on economic reality."

A similar approach has been followed in a number of recent cases holding that notes evidencing ordinary bank loans are not "securities" under federal law because they are issued in connection with "commercial," as opposed to "investment," transactions. See, e. g., C.N.S. Enterprises v. G. & G. Enterprises, 508 F.2d 1354 (7th Cir. 1975); but see Exchange Nat'l Bank v. Touche Ross & Co., 544 F.2d 1126 (2d Cir. 1976), rejecting the "commercial-investment" distinction.

(b) Financial Instruments

Most of the specialized types of investment instruments issued by financial institutions, such as life insurance policies and annuities, "shares" in savings and loan associations, or certificates of deposit in banks, are specifically exempted from the registration provisions (but not the antifraud provisions) of the federal securities laws. See SA § 3(a)(2), (5), (8); SEA § 3(a)(12). There is some question as to whether the traditional forms of these instruments would be deemed to be "securities" even in the absence of such exemption. However, when such institutions issue instruments on which the rate of return varies with the profitability of the institution or of a portfolio of securities, they will be considered "securities." The Supreme Court has held in two decisions that "variable annuities" issued by insurance companies are "securities" required to be registered under the 1933 Act. SEC v. Variable Annuity Life Ins. Co., 359 U.S. 65 (1959); SEC v. United Benefit Life Ins. Co., 387 U.S. 202 (1967). It has also held that withdrawable capital shares issued by a savings and loan association are "securities" for the purposes of the anti-fraud provisions of the 1934 Act, even though they are specifically exempted from the registration provisions of the 1933 Act. Tcherepnin v. Knight, 389 U.S. 332 (1967).

(c) Investment Contracts

The area of greatest difficulty has been in determining whether investments in a variety of money-raising schemes are "securities," even though there is no "note, stock, * * * or instrument commonly known as a 'security.'" The question has been whether an investment in such a scheme may nevertheless be an "investment contract" or a "certificate of interest or participation in any profit-sharing agreement." These terms have been liberally interpreted by the courts to apply to a wide range of schemes, particularly where the SEC or state regulators have sought injunctions against activities for which there was no prompt or effective relief available under other laws designed to protect the public.

Among the types of interests which have been held in certain circumstances to be "securities" are interests in oil and gas drilling programs, real estate condominiums and cooperatives, farm lands or animals, commodity option contracts, whiskey warehouse receipts, and multi-level distributorship arrangements and mechandise marketing schemes.

The basic test laid down by the Supreme Court in SEC v. W. J. Howey Co., 328 U.S. 293 (1946), is whether "the person invests his money in a common enterprise and is led to expect profits solely from the efforts of the promoter or a third party." In that case, the sale of individual rows of orange trees, in conjunction with a service contract under which the seller cultivated, harvested and marketed the orange crop, was held to involve a "security" within the meaning of the 1933 Act.

The *Howey* requirement that profits come "solely" from the efforts of others has led to decisions holding the securities laws inapplicable to franchise arrangements where the investor takes an active part in the business. See, e. g., Wieboldt v. Metz, 355 F.Supp. 255 (S.D.N.Y.1973). However, recent decisions have modified the interpretation of the word "solely" to reach fraudulent pyramid sales schemes in which the investor does have to exert some "efforts" in soliciting other persons to participate in the scheme, but where "the efforts made by those other than the investor are the undeniably significant ones, those essential managerial efforts which affect the failure or success of the enterprise." SEC v. Glenn W. Turner Enterprises, 474 F.2d 476 (9th Cir. 1973); see SEC v. Koscot Interplanetary, 497 F.2d 473 (5th Cir. 1974).

Some state courts, in construing their securities laws, have followed the lead of the California Supreme Court in Silver Hills Country Club v. Sobieski, 55 Cal.2d 811, 13 Cal.Rptr. 186, 361 P. 2d 906 (1961) and found a "security" even where the investor takes an active role in the enterprise, if the funds he contributes are part of the "risk capital" for the initial development of the business. Hawaii adopted a comparable, but more elaborate rule, in State v. Hawaii Market Center, 52 Haw. 642, 485 P.2d 105 (1971). In United Housing Foundation v. Forman, *supra*, the U.S. Supreme Court expressly declined to decide whether the "risk capital" test should be used in interpreting federal securities law.

(d) Exempt Securities

SA § 3(a) and SEA § 3(a)(12) contain lists of "exempted securities". In general, an "exempted security" is not subject to the registration and disclosure requirements of the particular statute, but may be subject to the general antifraud and civil liability provisions. While provisions of the

1933 Act do not apply to exempted securities "except as * * * expressly provided" (see, e. g., SA §§ 12(1) and 17(c)), provisions of the 1934 Act do apply to exempted securities unless their operation is specifically excluded (see, e. g., SA §§ 12(a) and 15(a)(1)).

The most important class of "exempted securities" under SA § 3(a)(2) and SEA § 3(a)(12) consists of obligations issued or guaranteed by the United States government or by state or local governments (including tax-exempt industrial development bonds). The 1933 Act (but not the 1934 Act) also exempts securities issued by banks, religious and other charitable organizations, savings and loan associations, and common carriers subject to regulation by the Interstate Commerce Commission, as well as bankruptcy certificates, and insurance policies and annuity contracts. Short-term (less than 9-month maturity) notes issued for working capital purposes and commonly known as "commercial paper" are "exempted securities" under SA § 3(a)(3) and are not a "security" under SEA § 3(a)(10).

The 1933 Act also exempts from its provisions certain "classes" of securities which are in reality transaction exemptions. Among these are securities issued in exchange for other securities (§§ 3(a)(9) and (10)) or in intrastate offerings (§ 3(a)(11)), as well as in small offerings made in compliance with SEC rules under § 3(b). (See § 10 *infra.*)

Proposals have recently been made (and, in some cases, adopted) to delete or restrict certain of these exemptions. The collapse of Penn Central Company in 1970 led to a reexamination of the exemptions for commercial paper and for securities of common carriers registered with the ICC. The Securities Exchange Act was amended in 1974 to require the banking agencies, which administer that Act's disclosure requirements with respect to bank securities, to conform their regulations to those of the SEC, unless different treatment could be justified. The Securities Acts Amendments of 1975 required firms that deal solely in state and local government securities to register with the SEC and to comply with rules laid down by a newly-created Municipal Securities Rulemaking Board, and bills have been introduced to require major state and local government issuers to distribute annual financial reports and to prepare "distribution statements" meeting SEC requirements in connection with their new offerings.

Application of the securities laws to certain kinds of "exempt" securities may raise difficult constitutional questions. In SEC v. World Radio Mission, 544 F.2d 535 (1st Cir. 1976), a religious organization claimed that an SEC action for an injunction against its sale of "loan plans" violated its freedom of religion under the First Amendment. The court held, however, that, since the loan plans were marketed to the general public and by appeal to economic motives rather than purely religious motives, they were outside the scope of First Amendment protection.

In City of Philadelphia v. SEC, CCH ¶ 96,073 (E.D.Pa.1977), a municipality alleged that a preliminary investigation by the SEC into alleged fraud in the issuance of its securities was an impermissible infringement on state sovereignty under the decision in National League of Cities v. Usery, 426 U.S. 833 (1976). The court held that the city had standing to challenge the SEC, but that the indirect harm to the city's credit caused by the existence of the investigation was not a direct enough interference with state or local government functions to bring the *Usery* rule into play.

II. REGULATION OF PUBLIC OFFERINGS

The process by which a corporation or other issuer offers and sells its securities to the public has been a principal focus of regulatory activity in the securities field. A major portion of the work of the SEC (and of lawyers engaged in securities practice) is devoted to registration of such offerings under the Securities Act of 1933 or in determining when such registration is required. While some people feel that there has been undue emphasis on this activity—to the detriment of other problem areas—the concepts and practices under the 1933 Act have lent a distinctive approach and tone to American securities regulation in general.

Unlike many state securities laws, the 1933 Act is essentially a "disclosure" statute. The SEC has no authority to decide whether a particular security may be offered to the public; it can only insist that the issuer make full disclosure of all material facts.

The heart of the 1933 Act is § 5, which provides in general that no security may be offered or sold to the public unless it is registered with the SEC. SA §§ 6 and 8 set forth the procedure for registration, and §§ 7 and 10 specify the information which must be disclosed. SA §§ 3 and 4 list types of securities and types of transactions which are exempt from the registration requirement.

Civil liability for damages is established by SA §§ 11 and 12. § 11 sets forth in detail the liabilities arising from misstatements or omissions in a registration statement, § 12(1) establishes civil liability for offers or sales in violation of § 5, and § 12(2) establishes liability for misstatements or omissions in any offer or sale of securities, whether or not registered under the Act. The only other substantive provision of the Act is § 17, which makes it unlawful to engage in fraudulent or deceitful practices in connection with any offer or sale of securities, whether or not registered under the Act.

§ 7. 1933 Act Disclosure Requirements

The basic purpose of the Securities Act of 1933 is to assure the availability of adequate reliable information about securities which are offered to the public. To achieve this objective, the Act makes it illegal to offer or sell securities to the public unless they have been registered. An issuer can register securities by filing with the SEC a "registration statement" containing certain information specified in the Act and in the SEC's rules and forms. Unlike registration under the 1934 Act, which covers an entire class of securities, registration under the 1933 Act covers only the securities actually being offered, and only for the purposes of the offering described in the registration statement. In other words, securities which have been registered under the 1933 Act for purposes of a public offering may have to be registered again if they are being reoffered in a new transaction subject to the registration requirements (such as a distribution of a "controlling" block of shares).

The "registration statement" consists of two parts: the "prospectus", a copy of which must be furnished to every purchaser of the securities, and "Part II", containing information and exhibits which need not be furnished to purchasers but are available for public inspection in the Commission's files.

SA § 7, by reference to Schedule A of the Act (or Schedule B, in the case of securities issued by foreign governments), prescribes the information to be included in a registration statement. § 10 (a)(1) specifies which of those items of information must be included in the prospectus furnished to purchasers.

SA § 7 authorizes the Commission (a) to require any additional information to be included in a registration statement or (b) to permit the omission of certain items of information with respect to particular classes of securities or issuers. Acting under this authority, the Commission has promulgated a number of different forms for registering different types of offerings, including Form S–2 (for companies in the developmental stage), S–5 (for mutual funds), S–7 (for companies meeting certain tests of stability and earning power), S–8 (for offerings to employees), and S–16 (for certain secondary offerings). The basic form for registration statements, however, is Form S–1, prescribed for use in all offerings for which no other form is authorized or prescribed.

The information required to be included in Form S–1 falls into four general categories:

	Items
The Method of Offering	1, 2, 4, 22, 23, 26
Description of the Security	13, 14, 15
The Issuer and Its Business	
Financial Statements	5, 6, 21, 30
Other Information	3, 7, 9, 10, 12, 27, 28
Management and Control	8, 11, 16, 17, 18, 19, 20, 24, 25

Supplementing the items and instructions contained in the forms themselves is the Commission's Regulation C, consisting of SA Rules 400–494, which prescribes registration procedures and the general form of registration statements and prospectuses. In addition, the Commission in 1968 published a set of "Guides for Preparation and Filing of Registration Statements," which "are not rules of the Commission" but "represent policies and practices followed by the Commission's Division of Corporation Finance in the administration of the registration requirements of the Act."

These rules, forms, and guides, however, are only the starting point in the preparation of a registration statement. The supposed objective of the 1933 Act is to produce a document which tells a prospective purchaser the things he really ought to know before buying a security. This objective, however, is not easy to attain. Among the factors which inhibit it are (1) the fact that it may be against the issuer's financial interest to tell investors the real weaknesses of the operation (it is much easier to prohibit a person from doing something wrong than to require him to do something well when he doesn't want to do it at all), and (2) the difficulty of putting complex financial arrangements or economic factors into language simple enough for the average investor to understand.

The task is complicated further by uncertainty as to whether the principal purpose of disclosure under the federal securities laws is to protect investors against really bad deals by making sure that negative factors are emphasized, or to enable them to make rational choices among alternative respectable deals by requiring a balanced presentation of affirmative and negative factors.

The SEC has traditionally taken the position that 1933 Act registration statements should contain only "hard" information, such as descriptions of current or completed activities and financial statements covering past periods. It has objected to inclusion of such "soft" information as appraisals of property and estimates of future earnings. These attitudes are currently being modified in light of disclosure problems under the 1934 Act.

§ 8. The Registration Process

Under SA § 8(a), a registration statement automatically becomes "effective" 20 days after it is filed with the Commission, at which point the issuer is free to sell the registered securities to the public. The Commission, however, has certain powers to delay or suspend the effectiveness of the registration statement. Under § 8(b), it can issue an order "refusing to permit such statement to become effective" if it appears that the statement "is on its face incomplete or inaccurate in any material respect." Under § 8(d), it can issue a "stop order" suspending the effectiveness of a registration statement which it finds to contain a misstatement or omission of a material fact.

In practice, the SEC has not used the "refusal order" at all (because of timing and procedural problems), and has used the "stop order" only in egregious situations. Strangely enough, the "stop order" proceeding is almost never used to "stop" an ongoing sale of securities under a registration statement which has just become effective. It is normally employed either (a) to prevent a registration statement with serious deficiencies from becoming effective, or (b) to publicize the deficiencies in a registration statement under which securities have already been publicly distributed. See, e. g., Universal Camera Corp. 19 S.E.C. 648 (1945); Franchard Corp., 42 S.E.C. 163 (1964).

This is not to say, however, that the SEC has played a passive role with respect to the contents of the great majority of registration statements filed with it. On the contrary, a substantial part of the time and energy of its staff has been devoted to the review of registration statements and the communication of the staff's views in "letters of comment," also known as "deficiency letters". In these informal communications, which are not provided for in the Act, the staff may insist on or suggest changes, additions or deletions, or may request additional information as a prelude to further comments.

The basis of this procedure, and of the willingness of issuers to go along with it, is SA § 8(a), which authorizes the Commission, subject to stated criteria, to permit a registration statement to become effective less than 20 days after filing. The issuer or underwriters making a distribution normally want to start selling the security as soon as they have set the price and other terms of the offering, which are usually omitted from the registration statement as originally filed. The inclusion of this information requires the filing of an amendment to the registration statement. Because § 8(a) provides that the filing of any amendment starts the 20-day period running again, the SEC's willingness to "accelerate" the effective date is crucial to every issuer which wants to proceed with its offering as soon as possible after filing the "price amendment."

In determining whether to grant "acceleration", the Commission is required to give "due regard to the adequacy of the information * * * available to the public, to the facility with which the nature of the securities * * * and the rights of holders thereof can be understood, and to the public interest and the protection of investors." In general, the Commission's decisions on acceleration rest on the issuer's willingness to make additions, deletions or modifications in the registration statement requested by the Commission staff (or to convince the Commission staff that they are inappropriate). However, in a "Note" to SA Rule 460, the Commission set down certain substantive conditions for acceleration, most notably a requirement that the issuer undertake not to indemnify its officers and directors against 1933 Act liability in the absence of a court determination that such indemnification would not contravene the public policy of the Act. This condition, which the Commission justified under the "public interest and protection of investors" test, has been criticized by members of the securities bar as an unwarranted extension of the Commission's discretionary power of acceleration.

From time to time, particularly when there is a heavy volume of 1933 Act filings, the Commission has announced that it will give only "cursory" or "summary" review to registration statements which appear to present no special problems, and will automatically accelerate the effective date to the date requested by the issuer. Several commentators have consistently urged the Commission to abandon its "letter of comment" procedure altogether and "permit the Securities Act of 1933 to operate in the manner in which it was originally written."

§ 9. The Operation of § 5

As noted above, the purpose of the 1933 Act is to prevent the public offering and sale of securities unless adequate information about them has been made available. The basic provisions designed to prevent such offers and sales are the prohibitions found in § 5 of the Act. In trying to understand the operation of § 5, you may find it helpful to keep in mind two basic patterns. The first is the sequence of participation in the movement of securities from the issuer to the public.

ISSUER⟫→ UNDERWRITERS⟫→ DEAL-ERS⟫→ PUBLIC

This is not always the pattern, but it is the one on which the basic restrictions and liabilities in the 1933 Act are based. An "underwriter" is defined as a person "who has purchased from an issuer with a view to, or offers or sells for an issuer in connection with, the distribution of any security or participates * * * in any such undertaking," but does not include a dealer "whose interest is limited to a commission [or discount] from an underwriter or dealer not in excess of the usual or customary distributors' or sellers' commission [or discount]." A "dealer" is a person who engages, as agent or principal, in the business of offering, buying or selling securities issued by another person.

In the normal "firm-commitment" underwriting, the underwriters purchase the securities as principal from the issuer and resell them to dealers for retail sale to the public. For example, the issuer may sell shares to the underwriters at $22, to be resold to dealers at $23, for reoffering to the public at $24. (A "firm-commitment" underwriting usually involves a "fixed-price" offering in which each dealer agrees to make a bona fide public offering at the price stated in the prospectus.) In a "best-efforts" underwriting, the underwriters simply agree to try to sell as many securities as they can, receiving a commission from the issuer for the securities sold.

The second basic pattern to keep in mind is the time sequence established by the 1933 Act, by reference to the date on which the registration statement is filed and the date on which it becomes "effective".

	FILING DATE	EFFECTIVE DATE	
PRE-FILING PERIOD	WAITING PERIOD	POST-EFFECTIVE PERIOD

SA § 5 has a dual thrust: (a) to prevent or restrict any public statements about the securities being offered, except those contained in the registration statement and the statutory prospectus, and (b) to assure that the statutory prospectus is made available to the investing public. Unfortunately, the structure of § 5 does not clearly reflect this division; nor does it clearly reflect the distinctions between the three different periods defined by the filing date and effective date of the registration statement. As an aid to your understanding of the structure of § 5, the following diagram indicates the respective periods in which the prohibitions contained in the five subdivisions of the section are applicable:

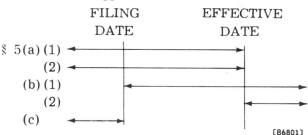

[B6801]

The complex structure of § 5 results from the 1954 amendments to the Securities Act. Prior to that time, the definition of "sale" in § 2(3) included offers as well as actual sales, so that § 5(a) prohibited any sales or offers prior to the effective date of the registration statement. The purpose of the 1954 amendments was to legitimate, and indeed encourage, the use of the preliminary or "red herring" prospectus to make written offers during the waiting period. Thus, § 5(c) now prohibits any offers prior to the filing of the registration statement, § 5(a) prohibits any sales prior to the effective date, § 5(b)(2) prohibits the delivery of a security after sale unless it is accompanied by the statutory prospectus, and § 5 (b)(1) prohibits the use of any prospectus which does not meet the requirements of § 10 (§ 10 having also been amended in 1954 to specify what information could be omitted from the preliminary prospectus used during the waiting period).

(a) The Pre-Filing Period

SA § 5(c) prohibits any offer to sell or offer to buy before a registration statement is filed. The definition of "offer" in § 2(3), however, exempts preliminary negotiations or agreements between the issuer and the underwriters or among underwriters, so that they may commence to negotiate the terms of the offering during that period. No offer may be made to dealers during this period, and dealers are also prohibited from offering to buy the securities, so that they cannot be pressured into trying to obtain priority for their orders before any reliable information is available.

The SEC takes a very broad view of what constitutes an "offer" for purposes of § 5(c). In addition to formal offers, any unusual publicity by the issuer or prospective underwriters about the issuer's business, or the prospects of the industry in which it is engaged, "may in fact contribute to conditioning the public mind or arousing public interest in the issuer or in the securities of an issuer in a manner which raises a serious question whether the publicity is not in fact part of the selling effort." SA Rel. 3844 (1957). In Carl M. Loeb, Rhoades & Co., 38 S.E.C. 843 (1959), the Commission held that underwriters had violated § 5(c) by issuing a press release about a proposed offering of a Florida land development company, and that the "news" value of the offering did not justify the release.

In recognition of the fact that publicly-held companies may have an obligation to make prompt disclosure of important developments, SA Rule 135 permits an issuer to put out a press release or other written notice of an offering that sets forth no more than the name of the issuer and the purpose and basic terms of the offering (without naming the underwriters). SA Rules 137–139, adopted in 1970, also permit broker-dealers to publish certain types of recommendations of securities, even when securities of the same issuer are currently being publicly distributed. However, in certain complex situations, such as an exchange offer by one company of its securities to shareholders of another company, an issuer may be found to have violated § 5(c) by making statements about its securities that it considered itself bound to make under the disclosure provisions of the 1934 Act. See Chris-Craft Industries v. Bangor Punta Corp., 426 F.2d 569 (2d Cir. 1970).

(b) The Waiting Period

As amended in 1954, § 5 permits offers, but not sales, during the waiting period between filing and effectiveness. There is no restriction on oral offers during this period. However, § 2(10) makes any offer in writing a "prospectus", and § 5(b)(1) makes it unlawful to transmit any prospectus after the filing of the registration statement unless the prospectus contains the information called for by § 10, some of which is generally unavailable until the underwriting agreements have been signed and the offering price has been set. To meet this problem, the Act and rules provide avenues for the use of two kinds of written offering material during the waiting period—the preliminary, or "red herring", prospectus, and the "tombstone ad."

SA § 10(b) provides that the Commission may permit for the purposes of § 5(b)(1) the use of a prospectus which omits or summarizes some of the information required by § 10(a). Pursuant to that authority, the Commission has adopted Rule 433, which provides that the offering price and related information may be omitted from a prospectus used prior to the effective date, but requires that a special legend must be printed in red (whence the name "red herring") on every such preliminary prospectus.

Acting under its general definitional power in SA § 19, the Commission has also adopted Rule 134, providing that the term "prospectus", as defined in § 2(10), will not include a notice which contains only certain specified information about the proposed issue, and also sets forth certain legends prescribed by the rule. Because of the black borders customarily placed around these notices, they are known as "tombstone ads."

While these provisions permit the dissemination of written information to potential investors during the waiting period, they do not require it. In the 1960's, the SEC became concerned about the fact that an offeree might never see a preliminary prospectus and not receive the final prospectus until after he had purchased the securities. In SA Rel. 4968 (1969), therefore, it announced that, before taking action to accelerate the effective date of a registration statement, it would require a written statement from the managing underwriter that copies of a preliminary prospectus had been mailed to all prospective purchasers at least 48 hours before the confirmations of sale were to be sent to them. It also adopted SEA Rule 15c2–8, under the antifraud provisions of the 1934 Act, requiring dealers to take reasonable steps to see that copies of the preliminary prospectus are made available to each salesman engaged in offering the securities and to any customer who makes a written request for one.

(c) The Post-Effective Period

After the registration statement becomes effective, underwriters and dealers are free to make offers and sales to anyone; the question is under what circumstances a copy of the final prospectus must be delivered to the purchaser. In general, a prospectus must be delivered (a) on any sale of securities which are part of the underwriters' original allotment which have not yet been publicly sold, and (b) on any resales by dealers, for a specified period after the commencement of the offering, of securities sold to the public and repurchased by the dealer. This results from the following complex of provisions.

SA § 5(b)(2), by its terms, requires that a prospectus be delivered on every sale of a security in interstate commerce. § 4(1), however, exempts sales by anyone who is not an "issuer, underwriter or dealer." § 4(3) exempts all sales by "dealers" (a term defined in § 2(12)), except for two classes of sales:

(1) the original sale by the dealer of the securities which are being distributed by the

issuer or by or through an underwriter, no matter how long the dealer has held them (§ 4(3)(C)); and

(2) resales by the dealer of securities which were sold to the public in such a distribution and reacquired by the dealer, but only if they take place within a specified period after the original public offering (§ 4(3)(A) and (B)).

The period specified in § 4(3) for the latter class of sales is forty days, in the case of securities of an issuer which has made a prior registered offering under the 1933 Act, and 90 days in the case of securities of an issuer which has not previously made a registered offering (§ 4(3), last sentence). However, the SEC, utilizing the exemptive power contained in that section, has adopted SA Rule 174, under which a dealer need not deliver a prospectus on any resale of a security of an issuer which is subject to the reporting requirements of the 1934 Act, no matter how soon after the public offering the resale takes place. For any issue in which dealers are required to deliver prospectuses on resale, SA Rule 425A requires that the prospectus set forth the date on which the requirement terminates.

The purpose of paragraph (A) of § 4(3) is to permit dealers to trade in a security which was illegally offered to the public without registration, after a lapse of 40 days from the time the offering was made. In Kubik v. Goldfield, 479 F.2d 472 (3d Cir. 1973), the court held that "for the purposes of determining a dealer exemption under § 4(3), a 'bona fide' offer to the public may occur when a stock first appears in the 'pink sheets', even though the stock may be 'illegally' unregistered."

If a dealer is required to deliver a prospectus a substantial time after the effective date, two problems may arise. First, § 10(a)(3) requires that any prospectus used more than nine months after the effective date be updated so that the information contained in it is not more than 16 months old. Second, whether or not nine months have elapsed, the dealer must be sure that the prospectus still contains an accurate and up-to-date description of the company. Delivery of a prospectus which is misleading at the time it is used may constitute a violation of SA § 17(a)(2) and subject the dealer to liability under SA § 12(2), even if the prospectus was completely accurate on the effective date. It may also constitute a violation of § 5(b)(2) subjecting the dealer to liability under SA § 12(1). SEC v. Manor Nursing Centers, 458 F.2d 1082 (2d Cir. 1972). A prospectus can be modified or supplemented to reflect events occurring after the effective date, provided 10 copies of the modified prospectus are filed with the SEC under SA Rule 424(c) before it is used.

§ 10. Exemptions from the 1933 Act

SA § 5, by its terms, requires registration for *any* sale by *any* person of *any* security, unless it is specifically exempted from the registration provisions by § 3 or § 4. §§ 3(a)(2)–(8) and 3(c) exempt certain kinds of securities from the registration requirements. §§ 3(a)(1), (9), (10), and (11), 3(b) and 4 exempt securities which are sold in certain kinds of transactions. The most important exemption in this latter category is § 4(1), which exempts "transactions by any person other than an issuer, underwriter or dealer." This provision, together with § 4(3), which exempts most transactions by dealers, effectively remove almost all secondary trading (i. e., trading in already outstanding securities) from the registration requirements of the Act. However, as set forth in the remainder of this section, there are some important exemptions for transactions which do involve the issuer, and there are some situations in which securities must be registered for sale even though they are being sold by someone other than the issuer.

(a) Private Placements

The most important exemption for an ordinary corporate issuer wishing to raise money without registration is the exemption in § 4(2) for "transactions by an issuer not involving any public offering." Very large amounts of securities have been sold pursuant to this exemption. Of the total of $41 billion of corporate securities offered for cash in 1972, according to SEC figures, nearly $11 billion was privately placed. In the years 1963–65 the volume of securities sold privately each year actually exceeded the volume sold in public offerings.

The vast bulk of these offerings, however, consists of "private placements" of large blocks of securities with institutional investors—typically the sale of notes or debentures to one or more insurance companies or pension funds. The SEC has generally raised no objections to the consummation of these transactions in reliance on the § 4(2) exemption, since the purchasers are customarily in a position to insist upon the issuer providing them with information more extensive than that contained in a registration statement and to give them other protections not available to purchasers in a registered public offering.

The private offering exemption is of course available for any other kind of offering which meets its basic criteria. Two areas where it has been effectively utilized are in offerings to key employees of the issuing company and in exchange offers to acquire the stock of closely-held companies.

The area of greatest difficulty has been the use of the § 4(2) exemption for promotional offerings to limited numbers of people. Restrictive interpretations by the SEC and the courts as to the manner in which, and the persons to whom, a "non-public" offering could be made, coupled with strict liability under SA § 12(1) if the terms of the exemption were not strictly complied with, made many lawyers dubious as to whether the § 4(2) exemption could ever be safely used in this situation. In an effort to bring some measure of certainty into this area, the SEC has recently adopted a new Rule 146, designed to provide more "objective" standards for the availability of the exemption.

In SEC v. Ralston Purina Co., 346 U.S. 119 (1953), the Supreme Court rejected the suggestion that the applicability of § 4(2) should depend on the number of persons to whom the offer was made, or the limitation of the offer to a defined class of persons (in that case, "key" employees of the issuer), and held that it should depend on whether the class of persons to whom the securities are being offered "need the protection of the Act." In the situation before it, the Court found that the employees involved "were not shown to have access to the kind of information which registration would disclose" and were therefore "entitled to compliance with § 5."

The SEC subsequently amplified the test enunciated by the Supreme Court, indicating that it would consider, among other things, the identity of the offerees and their relationship to the issuer, the size of the offering and of the units in which it was made, the use of investment bankers or stock exchange facilities, and the length of time for which the original purchasers held the securities. SA Rel. 4552 (1962). However, two restrictive decisions by the Fifth Circuit in 1971 and 1972 (including one in which the SEC took an extremely narrow view of the exemption) led to doubts as to whether the exemption would ever be available for offerings to small numbers of people to raise the initial capital for new ventures, unless the offerees had access to all material information about the issuer by virtue of their status as "insiders." Hill York Corp. v. American Int'l Franchises, 448 F.2d 680 (5th Cir. 1971); SEC v. Continental Tobacco Co., 463 F.2d 137 (5th Cir. 1972). These decisions intensified pressure for development of a more "objective" test of what constitutes a "private" offering exempt from 1933 Act registration requirements.

In April 1974, the SEC adopted SA Rule 146 to provide more "objective" standards. Under Rule 146, an offering will not be deemed to be "public" within the meaning of § 4(2) if:

(1) The securities are purchased by not more than 35 persons. (This is an important change from prior interpretations, under which the focus was on the number of offerees, rather than the number of pur-

chasers.) A person who purchases more than $150,000 of securities in the offering need not be counted in computing the number of purchasers; thus, a "private placement" can be made to any number of large institutions as long as each one invests $150,000 or more.

(2) There is no general advertising, and no oral or written solicitation of persons other than eligible offerees.

(3) The securities are offered and sold only to persons who the issuer has reason to believe (1) are sufficiently experienced to be able to evaluate the merits and risks of the investment, or (2) are able to bear the risk of the investment and, prior to the sale, have the services of a representative who has sufficient knowledge and experience to make such evaluation.

(4) Each offeree either has access to, or is furnished with, the kind of information that would be supplied in a registration statement. (This is a major change from prior law, under which it was not sufficient for the issuer to furnish information equivalent to what would be found in a registration statement; each offeree had to have a relationship with the issuer that gave him the power to *require* the furnishing of such information.)

(5) The issuer takes certain specified steps to assure that the securities are not resold by the purchasers, except in accordance with the rules governing such resales.

Rule 146 contains elaborate definitions and explanations of its various requirements, and the exemption is available only if all the requirements of the Rule are strictly complied with. Even if there is strict compliance, the rule is not available if the offering is "part of a plan or scheme to evade the registration provisions of the Act." Rule 146 is not the exclusive means of satisfying the requirements of § 4(2), however; an offering may still be considered "non-public" if it meets the standards laid down in SEC and court interpretations of that section. In that connection, the Fifth Circuit recently modified its interpretation of § 4(2) to correspond more closely to Rule 146, by holding that an issuer was entitled to the exemption if it could show that offerees either had access to, or were furnished with, the necessary information. Doran v. Petroleum Mgmt. Corp., 545 F.2d 893 (5th Cir. 1977).

(b) Intrastate Offerings

SA § 3(a)(11) exempts from the registration requirements of the 1933 Act "any security which is part of an issue offered and sold only to persons resident within a single State * * * where the issuer of such security is * * * a corporation incorporated by and doing business within such State." Note that this exemption is distinct from the jurisdictional provisions of the Act relating to use of facilities of interstate commerce; an offering may qualify for the intrastate exemption even if the mails or other interstate communication facilities are used, as long as the issuer and all the offerees and purchasers have the requisite connection with the state.

Because of the strict requirements of the exemption with respect to offerees, it is virtually useless for making public offerings except in isolated areas far from any state border. Not only each purchaser, but each offeree, must be a "resident" (usually defined as comparable to "domiciliary"), so that an offer to one non-resident can destroy the entire exemption. As far as the issuer is concerned, the SEC and the courts have construed the "doing business" requirement to mean not only that the issuer is doing some business in the state, but that it is doing "substantial" business in the state. See SEC v. Truckee Showboat, 157 F.Supp. 824 (S.D.Cal.1957); Chapman v. Dunn, 414 F.2d 153 (6th Cir. 1969). The SEC's basic position has been that the exemption was designed for "local financing for local industries, carried out through local investment." SA Rel. 4434 (1961).

To provide greater certainty for issuers in determining when the requirements of § 3(a)(11) are met, the Commission in 1974 adopted SA Rule 147, defining certain of the terms in that section. Under Rule 147, an issuer is deemed to be "doing business" in a state only if (a) it is deriving at least 80% of its gross revenues from the state, (b) has at least 80% of its assets in the state, (c) intends to use at least 80% of the proceeds of the offering in the state, and (d) has its principal office in the state. Also, in connection with the question whether the offering has "come to rest" within the state, or is merely the first step in an interstate distribution, Rule 147 provides that the offering will be considered "intrastate" if no resales are made to nonresidents of the state for a period of at least nine months after the initial distribution of the securities is completed.

(c) Small Offerings

Unlike the exemptions for non-public and intrastate offerings, which are set forth in the Act itself, § 3(b) authorizes the SEC, "by rules and regulations," to exempt other offerings, not exceeding $500,000 in amount, when it finds that registration is not necessary "by reason of the small amount involved or the limited character of the public offering." Under this authority, the Commission has adopted a number of rules providing exemptions for certain specialized kinds of offerings, such as oil and gas drilling programs.

In addition, it has adopted Regulation A (comprising SA Rules 251–263 and related forms), a general exemption for public offering of ordinary securities.

As it has developed over the years, Regulation A has become not so much an exemption as a simplified form of registration for small issues. Unlike the exemptions described above, it is not satisfied by a finding that specified conditions exist, but only upon compliance with procedures similar in many ways to the 1933 Act registration process.

Qualification for the Exemption. The principal criterion for availability of the exemption, of course, is that the total amount of all offerings by the issuer under Regulation A during any 12-month period may not exceed $500,000. If some of the securities are sold to "insiders" in the initial distribution, then the price at which they resell to "the public" is used in determining the aggregate offering price. See Shearson, Hammill & Co., 42 S.E.C. 811 (1965). And if the issuer is a promotional company without established earnings potential, Rule 253 requires that all of its securities held by directors, officers, promoters, underwriters or dealers must be counted in determining the aggregate offering price unless effective provisions are made to prevent them from being resold for at least one year after the offering.

While the issuer can offer up to $500,000 under Regulation A, a person other than the issuer (who otherwise is not free to sell without registration) can normally only utilize Regulation A to sell up to $100,000 of securities at any one time.

In addition to the quantity limitations, Rule 252 sets forth certain "good guy" qualifications. The exemption is not available if the issuer, underwriter, or any related persons have been convicted of securities offenses, subject to SEC disciplinary proceedings, or involved in certain other types of proceedings, within specified periods.

Procedure. To comply with the Regulation A exemption, the issuer must file a "notification" and "offering circular" with the SEC at least 10 days before the offering is to commence. The offering circular must contain information comparable to that required in a 1933 Act prospectus, but in much less detail, and with financial statements that may be unaudited. Unlike registration statements, which must be filed in Washington, the Regulation A filing is made at the SEC regional office for the area where the issuer has its principal place of business.

While Regulation A appears to give the issuer the right to start offering 10 days after filing, in practice the SEC follows the same "letter of comment" procedure that it follows with respect to registration statements, and issuers normally do not commence the offering until they have received and responded to the SEC comments.

Under Rule 256, a copy of the offering circular must be given to every person to whom a written offer is made or to whom a sale is confirmed. (The offering circular must be furnished at least 48 hours prior to confirmation, if the issuer is not subject to the periodic disclosure requirements of the 1934 Act.) Provisions for updating the offering circular, and for filing reports on the results of the offering, are also comparable to those for fully registered offerings.

The Regulation A notification and offering circular do not create any civil liabilities under SA § 11, but they do give rise to liability under SA § 12(2) for any misstatements or omissions.

Rule 240. To provide a simple exemption for very small offerings by issuers who cannot meet the technical requirements of the non-public or intrastate exemptions and do not want to go through the procedures of Regulation A, the Commission in 1975 adopted SA Rule 240. Under this rule, an issuer can sell up to $100,000 of securities in any 12-month period, provided that the sales do not result in the issuer's securities being held by more than 100 beneficial owners. There are no requirements as to the residence of the purchasers or their access to information about the issuer. However, no general solicitation, advertising, or sales commission is permitted, and resales by purchasers are restricted to the same extent as if they had purchased in private transactions under § 4(2). A report of all sales made under Rule 240 must be filed by the issuer with the appropriate SEC regional office for any year in which such sales are made. SA Rel. 5560 (1975).

(d) Mergers and Reorganizations

When an issuer offers securities, not for cash, but in exchange for other securities (issued either by itself or by another issuer), the offer and subsequent exchange are considered an "offer" and "sale" for purposes of the 1933 Act. The transaction may, of course, be exempt as a nonpublic or intrastate offering, or may be exempt under SA § 3(a)(9) (exchange by the issuer with its own security holders where no commission is paid to anyone for soliciting the exchange) or § 3(a)(10) (exchange approved after a hearing by a state bank or insurance commissioner or other governmental authority).

The Act does not make clear, however, whether there is an "offer" and "sale" when the exchange takes place pursuant to a merger, sale of assets, or recapitalization, under state corporation law, in which the favorable vote of a specified majority of the shareholders operates to authorize the transaction and obligate all shareholders to accept the exchange. For almost 40 years, the SEC took the position that no "sale" was involved in such a transaction, at least insofar as the registration requirements of § 5 were concerned, and that accordingly no registration statement had to be filed, and no prospectus had to be delivered to shareholders whose votes were solicited for approval of the merger or other transaction. (The SEC's proxy rules under the 1934 Act did require that the shareholders be furnished with detailed information about the proposed transaction if their securities were of a class registered under that Act.)

In 1972, the SEC reversed its long-standing position and adopted SA Rule 145, under which the solicitation of shareholders' votes for approval of a reclassification, merger or sale of assets is considered an "offer" for 1933 Act purposes, requiring the filing of a registration statement and delivery of a prospectus to each shareholder. To coordinate this new requirement with existing 1934 Act disclosure requirements, the Commission adopted a new Form S–14, in which the information called for is basically that which the issuer is or would be required to provide under the 1934 Act proxy regulations to the shareholders whose votes are being solicited. SA Rel. 5316 (1972).

"Spin-Offs" and *"Shell Corporations"*. The SEC has taken special steps to deal with two kinds of

"reorganizations" which promoters have used to distribute shares to the public without registration under the 1933 Act. See SA Rel. 4982 (1969). The "spin-off" involves the issuance by a company, with little or no business activity, of some of its shares to a publicly-owned company for a nominal consideration. The publicly-owned company then "spins off" the shares as a distribution to its shareholders, creating a public trading market into which the insiders can sell the remaining shares. The courts have held that the total transaction requires registration under the 1933 Act, even though the distribution to the shareholders of the public-owned company is not technically a "sale." SEC v. Datronics Engineers, 490 F.2d 250 (4th Cir. 1973); SEC v. Harwyn Industries, 326 F.Supp. 943 (S.D.N.Y.1971).

The "shell corporation" is one which has ceased active operations and has little or no assets, but has substantial amounts of stock held by members of the public. Promoters obtain control of the company, engage in a series of "acquisitions" or other transactions which cause the market price of the stock to rise dramatically, then take advantage of the inflated market to sell the shares that they have acquired. The courts have accepted the SEC's position that transactions of this type violate both the registration and antifraud provisions. See SEC v. North American Research & Dev. Corp., 424 F.2d 63 (2d Cir.

1970); SEC v. A. G. Bellin Securities Corp., 171 F.Supp. 233 (S.D.N.Y.1959).

(e) Sales by Persons Other than the Issuer

As noted above, SA § 4(1) exempts from the registration requirements "transactions by any person other than an issuer, underwriter or dealer" and § 4(3) exempts most transactions by dealers. Therefore, the only transactions not involving the issuer which require registration are those which involve an "underwriter."

The term "underwriter" is defined in § 2(11) as "any person who has purchased from an issuer with a view to, or offers or sells for an issuer in connection with, the distribution of any security * * * ". Solely for the purpose of this definition, the term "issuer" is defined to include any person who "controls" the issuer. "Control" is defined in SA Rule 405 as "the power to direct or cause the direction of the management and policies of a person, whether through the ownership of voting securities, by contract, or otherwise." Control is basically a question of fact; a particular corporation may be found to be controlled by one or a number of shareholders, by its chief executive officer, by some or all of its directors, or by some other person or combination.

Under these definitions, there are two types of transactions which may be found to involve an "underwriter", even though there is no investment banker performing the traditional functions of the "underwriter" in a formal public offering:

(1) when a person who "controls" an issuer sells securities of that issuer through a broker or dealer, the broker or dealer is deemed to be "selling for an *issuer*" and may therefore be an "underwriter";

(2) when a person has purchased securities directly from an issuer, and subsequently resells them, he may be deemed to have "purchased from an issuer with a view to distribution" and thus himself be an "underwriter."

The first situation was involved in Ira Haupt & Co., 23 S.E.C. 589 (1946). Schulte, who controlled Park & Tilford, sold a total of 93,000 shares of Park & Tilford through Haupt, his broker, in transactions on the New York Stock Exchange. The SEC asserted that the transactions should have been registered because Haupt was an "underwriter". Haupt argued that there was no "distribution"; Schulte had simply given a series of orders to sell 200 or 300 shares at a time. The SEC rejected this defense; the circumstances clearly put Haupt on notice that a "distribution" was intended. Haupt then argued that, even if it was an "underwriter", the transaction was exempt under § 4(4), which exempts "brokers' transactions executed upon customers' orders on any exchange * * *." The SEC held that this exemption did not apply to situations where the broker-dealer was an "underwriter", but was designed only to permit dealers to execute brokerage transactions for ordinary retail customers at a time when, as dealers, they might be prohibited from engaging in transactions for their own account.

The *Haupt* decision created great uncertainty as to how many shares a broker could sell for a "controlling person" without being involved in a "distribution". The Commission accordingly adopted SA Rule 154 (subsequently superseded by SA Rule 144), which provided that a sale by a broker for a "controlling person" would be exempt under § 4(4) if the broker carried out only the normal brokerage functions and had no reason to believe that the controlling person's aggregate sales over a six-month period exceeded a certain specified amount. The rule was designed only to protect the broker; a "controlling person" who effected a distribution through brokers violated the Act by selling through "underwriters", even though no individual broker may have been aware that the quantity limits of Rule 154 were being exceeded. U. S. v. Wolfson, 405 F.2d 779 (2d Cir. 1968).

The second type of situation arose in innumerable instances where people bought securities from an issuer in a private transaction and wished to resell them. Since the determination whether the person was an underwriter depended on whether he had "purchased * * * with a view to distribution," there had to be an examination of his subjective intent at the time of purchase, and a search for a "change in circumstances" that would justify him in selling now even though he had originally taken the securities "for investment." The brokerage transaction exemption of Rule 154 was not considered applicable to this type of situation, and the SEC took the position that holding the securities for two years, or even longer, did not satisfy the requirement of "investment intent." The Commission accordingly was deluged with requests for "no-action" letters permitting sales under specified factual conditions.

Finally, in 1972, the Commission adopted a new Rule 144, applying a relatively objective (if rather complex) set of rules to both types of "underwriter" transactions. SA Rel. 5223 (1972).

(1) The basic quantity restrictions found in Rule 154 were made applicable (with minor changes) to both kinds of transactions; a person's sales under Rule 144 during any six-month period may not exceed the lesser of (a) 1% of the total number of units of the security outstanding and (b) if the security is listed on an exchange, the

average weekly trading volume for the preceding four weeks.

(2) If the person acquired the securities from the issuer in a non-public transaction, he must have held them for at least two years before reselling them. (Securities are not considered fungible for this purpose; securities held for more than two years may be sold, even if the seller has recently acquired additional securities of the same class from the issuer.)

(3) The issuer must be subject to, and in current compliance with, the periodic reporting requirements of the 1934 Act, or there must otherwise be publicly available information comparable to that which would be found in such reports. (For issuers which do not meet this requirement, a much more limited resale exemption is provided by Rule 237, adopted at the same time as Rule 144.)

(4) The securities must be sold in ordinary brokerage transactions not involving any special remuneration or solicitation.

(5) A notice of each sale must be filed with the SEC at the time the order is placed with the broker.

The resale limitations of Rule 144 also apply to certain persons who receive securities in mergers or asset acquisitions, by virtue of SA Rule 145. Under Rule 145(c), controlling persons of an acquired company in a merger or sale of assets transaction are considered "underwriters" of the securities of the acquiring company which they acquire and subsequently resell in public transactions. Rule 145(d) permits such persons to resell without registration provided they comply with the quantity limitations and other restrictions of Rule 144 (except that they are not subject to the two-year holding period requirement).

(f) Problems Common to 1933 Act Exemptions

"Integration" of Offerings. In determining whether an offering qualifies for a particular exemption, it is necessary to determine whether it is in fact a separate offering, or whether it is part of a larger offering. This question often arises where an issuer, or a group of related issuers, engage in a series of "non-public" or "intrastate" offerings, or some combination thereof.

The SEC has stated that the factors to be considered in determining whether offerings should be "integrated" are whether the offerings (1) are part of a single plan of financing, (2) involve the same class of security, (3) are made at or about the same time, (4) involve the same type of consideration, and (5) are made for the same general purpose. SA Rel. 4552 (1963). In the case of non-public offerings, Rule 146 does not supply any more definite criteria. In the case of intrastate offerings, Rule 147 provides that offerings separated by a period of at least six months during which no offers or sales of that class of securities are made will not be integrated; if that test is not met, they are judged by the above criteria.

Under Regulation A, an issuer may sell up to the $500,000 limit each year, even if the successive financings are part of a prearranged plan. However, a closely related offering purportedly made pursuant to another exemption may reduce the maximum available under Regulation A if it would be considered part of the same offering under the SEC's enunciated criteria.

The limitations on sales by or through "underwriters" in Rule 144 also permit a prearranged program of sales, as long as the rolling six-month ceiling is not exceeded. However, the rule contains complicated provisions for "aggregating" sales by persons who have agreed to act in concert, or who have certain specified relationships to each other, in computing the maximum amount that may be sold.

Interrelationship of Exemptions. An offering must fall completely within a single exemption to escape registration. For example, an issuer cannot make a public offering in its home state simultaneously with "private" sales of the same security to selected residents of other states; if the offering is a single offering, it will be neither "intrastate" nor "private". On the other hand, an offering may qualify for more than one exemption. An issuer which is attempting to comply with the private offering exemption, but is not sure all the offerees meet the applicable standard, can protect itself by offering only to residents of its home state; the offering may be "intrastate" even if it is not "private".

Consequences of Noncompliance. The SEC and the courts have consistently held that the exemptions from the 1933 Act registration requirements are to be strictly construed, and that the person claiming the exemption has the burden of establishing all the facts necessary to support it. This burden is especially onerous because the exemption generally relates to the offering as a whole, rather than the transaction with each investor. Thus, if an offer is made to a single ineligible person in a "private" placement, or if one of the directors of the issuer was the subject of an SEC proceeding that disqualified the issuer from using Regulation A, the basis for the exemption is destroyed, and every offer or sale made by the issuer has violated § 5. Under § 12(1), any person who sells a security in violation of § 5 is liable to the purchaser to refund the full purchase price. A purchaser whose investment has gone down in value may therefore be able to recover his entire purchase price, without evidence of fraud or misstatement, if the seller is unable to establish the necessary conditions for the exemption on which it relied. See Henderson v. Hayden Stone, 461 F.2d 1069 (5th Cir. 1972).

§ 11. Civil Liability for Misstatements

While the prohibitions found in SA § 5 are designed to assure that securities will not be offered to the public without registration, sanctions are necessary to assure that the information contained in the registration statement is complete and accurate.

The most powerful incentive to careful preparation of the registration statement is found in SA § 11, which sets forth the civil liabilities to purchasers with respect to any material misstatements or omissions. In contrast to the vague outlines of common law fraud liability, § 11 sets forth in great detail who may sue, what they must show, who can be held liable for how much, and the defenses and cross-claims available to various classes of defendants.

SA § 11 was considered such a draconian measure at the time of its enactment that some observers thought that it would dry up the nation's underwriting business and that "grass would grow in Wall Street." It is somewhat ironic, therefore, (or perhaps simply a testimonial to the care with which people approached the task of preparing registration statements) that the first fully litigated decision interpreting the civil liability provisions of § 11 did not come until 35 years later, after more than 27,000 registration statements had become effective, covering offerings to the public of more than $384 billion of securities. When that decision did come down, however, in Escott v. BarChris Construction Corp., 283 F.Supp. 643 (S.D.N.Y.1968), it spread new waves of concern among issuers, directors, underwriters, and their counsel and accountants, as they realized that the practices that had been followed during the new-issue boom of the early 1960's simply did not measure up to the standard of "due diligence" laid down in § 11.

Because § 11 liability is a matter of such overriding concern, it is a major influence in deciding what provisions and conditions will be included in the agreement between the issuer and underwriters, and in assigning responsibilities to the various parties involved in the registration statement. Any lawyer involved in underwriting work, therefore, should have a precise knowledge of the provisions of the section, how they have been interpreted, and how they relate to the other civil liability provisions of the federal securities laws.

The provisions of § 11, which apply only to offerings registered under the 1933 Act, are supplemented by the civil liability provisions of § 12, which apply to all sales of securities. The differences and interrelationships between § 11 and §

12(2) liabilities are also considered in this section.

(a) Elements of a § 11 Claim

In basic outline, § 11 provides that if a registration statement, at the time it became effective, "contained an untrue statement of a material fact or omitted to state a material fact required to be stated therein or necessary to make the statements therein not misleading," any person who acquired any security covered by the registration statement can sue certain specified persons to recover the difference between the price he paid for the security (but not more than the public offering price) and the price at which he disposed of it or (if he still owns it) its value at the time of suit.

Who Can Sue?   Section 11 gives a right of action to "any person acquiring such security" (there is no direct antecedent for the "such", but the courts have construed it as meaning any security registered by that registration statement). He need not have purchased it in the course of the original distribution; he will still have a right of action if he purchased it in a secondary transaction after it had already been publicly sold. (If this were not so, defendants could avoid all liability if the original purchasers all resold their securities at a profit, and the price subsequently went down when the misstatements in the registration statement became known.)

However, if the registration statement covers additional securities of a class which is already publicly traded, plaintiff must show that the securities he bought in a secondary transaction were part of the block sold in the new offering, and not part of those previously outstanding. Barnes v. Osofsky, 373 F.2d 269 (2d Cir. 1967). This can pose an insuperable obstacle to plaintiffs in the case of securities listed on a stock exchange, where there is usually no way for a buyer to ascertain the identity of the person who sold the securities to him.

Materiality and Reliance. All that the purchaser must show to recover is (a) that there was a material misstatement or omission in the registration statement and (b) that he lost money. Normally he need not show that he relied on the misstatement or omission, or even that he received a copy of the prospectus. However, if he purchased the security *after* the issuer had made generally available an earning statement covering a period of at least 12 months *beginning after* the effective date of the registration statement, he must show reliance on the misstatement or omission, but his reliance can be established without showing that he actually read the registration statement. SA § 11(a).

The term "material" is defined in SA Rule 405 as meaning "matters as to which an average prudent investor ought reasonably to be informed before purchasing the security registered." This has been construed for § 11 purposes as meaning "a fact which if it had been correctly stated or disclosed would have deterred or tended to deter the average prudent investor from purchasing the securities in question." Escott v. BarChris Construction Corp., *supra.*

Affirmative Defenses. Under § 11(a), a claim made by any purchaser can be defeated if the defendant can show that the purchaser knew of the untruth or omission at the time he acquired the security.

Under § 11(e), a claim may be defeated or reduced to the extent that the defendant can show that the decline in value of the security resulted from causes other than the misstatement or omission in the registration statement. Thus, if a defendant can show that a decline in the value of the issuer's securities was comparable to that suffered by other companies in the same industry (particularly if it occurred before the misstatement or omission in the registration statement was revealed), it may escape liability for that decline. See Beecher v. Able, CCH ¶ 95,016 (S.D. N.Y.1975). On the other hand, where the issuer has gone bankrupt for reasons unrelated to the misstatements or omissions in the registration statement, that fact alone should not completely defeat a purchaser's right of action; he should still be able to recover the difference between what he paid and what the securities would have been worth at the time of purchase if adequate disclosure had been made.

(b) Persons Liable

SA § 11(a) entitles the purchaser to sue (a) every person who signed the registration statement (§ 6 requires that it be signed by the issuer itself, by the principal executive, financial and accounting officers, and by a majority of the board of directors), (b) every director, (c) every person who has consented to being named as a director or prospective director, (d) every accountant, engineer, appraiser or other expert who has consented to being named as having prepared or certified a part of the registration statement, and (e) every underwriter.

All of these persons are made jointly and severally liable (i. e. a purchaser can sue any one of them to recover his entire damages) with two exceptions. An expert is only liable with respect to misstatements or omissions in the portion of the registration statement that he prepared or certified. And the aggregate liability of an underwriter who purchased only a portion of the issue (and who did not receive any special compensation from the issuer) is limited to the aggregate

public offering price of the securities which it un-
derwrote. (For example, in a public offering of
1,000,000 shares at $10 a share, if each of 10 un-
derwriters agrees, *severally and not jointly*, to
purchase 100,000 of the shares, § 11(e) limits the
liability of each underwriter to $1,000,000.)

The "Due Diligence" Defense. Except as to
the issuer, which has absolute liability for any
material misstatements or omissions, § 11(b)
provides an affirmative defense for any other defendant who can demonstrate that he met a prescribed standard of diligence with respect to the
information contained in the registration statement. For this purpose, the registration statement is divided into two portions: the "expertised" and the "unexpertised" portions. The "expertised" portions are those "purporting to be
made on the authority of an expert," i. e., those
specifically referred to in the expert's certificate
or opinion included in the registration statement.
The court in the *BarChris* case rejected the suggestion that the lawyers who prepared the main
body of the registration statement were "experts"
for purposes of § 11, or that the accountants had
"expertised" any parts of the registration statement other than their audited financial statements.

With respect to the "expertised" portions of
the registration statement, the "due diligence"
obligation of any defendant (other than the "ex-

pert" who prepared that portion) is worded negatively: that "he had no reasonable ground to believe and did not believe" that there was any material misstatement or omission. With respect to the "unexpertised" portions (and with respect to the liability of the "expert" for the portion he has "expertised") the obligation is worded affirmatively: that "he had, after reasonable investigation, reasonable ground to believe and did believe" that there was no material misstatement or omission.

Section 11(c) provides that "in determining * * * what constitutes reasonable investigation and reasonable ground for belief, the standard of reasonableness shall be that required of a prudent man in the management of his own property." The *BarChris* decision made clear that a defendant could not establish that he had made a "reasonable investigation" by showing that he had relied on others to do his investigating for him. However, it also indicated that the type and extent of investigation required to establish the "due diligence" defense of any particular defendant would depend on his area of expertise and his relationship to the issuer. For example, a lawyer-director engaged in the preparation of the registration statement would be expected to examine all corporate minutes, contracts and other legal documents, while a non-lawyer "outside" director would not normally be expected to do so.

PUBLIC OFFERINGS §

Subsequent commentary and decisions have indicated that "inside" directors—those having intimate knowledge of corporate affairs and transactions—may find it virtually impossible to establish their "due diligence" and that "their liability approaches that of the issuer as guarantor of the accuracy of the prospectus." Feit v. Leasco, 332 F.Supp. 544 (E.D.N.Y.1971).

Indemnification and Contribution. Many state corporation laws, as well as corporate charters or by-laws, permit or require corporations to indemnify their officers and directors against liabilities they may incur in the conduct of their corporate functions. Underwriting agreements customarily contain provisions under which the issuer and the underwriters agree to indemnify each other with respect to liability for misstatements in the portions of the registration statement for which each was primarily responsible.

The SEC has taken the position that it would be against public policy for an issuer to indemnify any officer, director or controlling person (or any underwriter with which any such person was affiliated) against 1933 Act liabilities. It has made a practice of refusing to accelerate the effective date of registration statements unless the issuer undertakes to submit the question to a court before making any indemnification payment in these circumstances. See Note to SA

Rule 460. However, after 43 years, the precise question has yet to be judicially determined.

The closest approach to a resolution came in Globus v. Law Research Service, 418 F.2d 1276 (2d Cir. 1969). In that case an underwriter sought contractual indemnification from the issuer for liability it had incurred under SA § 12(2) as a result of misstatements in an offering circular used in an offering that was exempt from the 1933 Act registration requirements. The court held that the public policy enunciated by the SEC barred the underwriter from recovering indemnification under its contract, where it was found to have had "actual knowledge" of the misstatements. The court's holding was thus broader than the SEC's position in denying indemnification to an underwriter which had no other affiliation with the issuer; on the other hand, it purported only to deal with the situation where the person seeking indemnification had "committed a sin graver than ordinary negligence."

With respect to contribution, § 11(f) provides that any person held liable may recover contribution from others who could have been held similarly liable, unless the person seeking contribution was, and the other was not, guilty of fraudulent misrepresentation. In subsequent proceedings in the *Globus* case, the court followed that approach under § 12(2). Globus v. Law Research Service, 318 F.Supp. 955 (S.D.N.Y.1970).

(c) Liability Under § 12(2)

Supplementing the very specific civil liability provisions of § 11 is § 12(2), which imposes liability on any person who offers or sells securities by means of any written or oral communication which misstates a material fact or omits a material fact necessary to make the statements made not misleading under the circumstances. The purchaser of the securities (provided he did not know of the untruth or omission) may sue to recover the consideration paid.

While the basic standard of liability in § 12(2) is similar to that set forth in § 11, its scope is entirely different. It applies to misstatements or omissions in any form, in any transaction, whether or not subject to the registration provisions of the 1933 Act. On the other hand, the purchaser must show that the security was actually offered or sold to him by means of the communication which contained the misstatement or omission, and he can sue only the person who actually sold the security to him. The seller has an affirmative defense if he can establish that he did not know, and in the exercise of reasonable care could not have known, of the untruth or omission. If a broker-dealer represents that it has investigated the creditworthiness of an issuer whose securities it sells, it can be held liable under § 12(2) if it was not diligent in making that investigation. University Hill Fdtn. v. Goldman, Sachs & Co., 422 F.Supp. 879 (S.D.N.Y.1976).

III. REGULATION OF PUBLICLY–HELD COMPANIES

§ 12. Overview of the 1934 Act

Unlike the Securities Act of 1933, which focuses largely on a single provision, and has been amended only slightly since its enactment, the Securities Exchange Act of 1934 contains provisions dealing with a number of different areas and has been subject to very substantial amendments and additions, most notably in 1964, 1968 and 1975. The scope and organization of the Act can best be understood by reference to the following table of sections:

I. SECURITIES AND EXCHANGE COMMISSION   **Section**

    A. Establishment and Constitution   4

    B. Investigations and Injunctions   21

    C. Conduct of Hearings   22

    D. Rules and Regulations   23

    E. Public Availability of Information   24

    F. Court Review of Orders and Rules   25

VII. SCOPE AND JURISDICTION

Sections 12, 13, 14 and 16 of the Securities Exchange Act impose disclosure and other requirements on publicly-traded companies.

SEA § 12 requires any issuer which has a class of securities traded on a national securities exchange to register with the SEC. (This registration of a class of securities under the 1934 Act must be distinguished from registration of an offering of securities under the 1933 Act; a company which has registered a class of securities under the 1934 Act will still have to register a particular offering of securities of that class under the 1933 Act if the provisions of that Act so require.) In 1964, § 12(g) was added, extending the registration requirements to any company which has total assets exceeding $1,000,000 and a class of equity securities with at least 500 shareholders of record.

SEA § 12(j) empowers the SEC to revoke or suspend the registration of a security, after notice and opportunity for hearing, if it finds that the issuer has violated any provision of the 1934 Act or the rules and regulations under it. Under SEA § 12(k), the SEC can summarily suspend trading in any security for a period of not more than 10 days, or, with the approval of the President, suspend all trading in all securities for a period of not more than 90 days. Prior to 1975, the SEC often imposed successive 10-day suspensions that prohibited trading in a particular security for months or even years at a time, when the Commission felt there was inadequate public information to enable investors to make an intelligent judgment as to the value of the stock. However, in Sloan v. SEC, 547 F.2d 152 (2d Cir. 1976), the court held the statute, as amended in 1975, did not authorize the SEC to impose successive 10-day suspensions of a particular security for more than 90 days in total; longer suspensions require notice and an opportunity for hearing.

SEA § 13 requires every issuer which has securities registered under § 12 to file periodic and other reports with the SEC, and § 14 regulates the solicitation of proxies from holders of such securities, in each case subject to rules prescribed by the SEC. Sections 13(d) and (e) and 14(d), (e) and (f), added by the "Williams Act" in 1968, regulate take-over bids, tender offers and purchases by companies of their own shares.

Section 16 requires every officer, director and 10% shareholder of an issuer which has securities registered under § 12 to report his purchases and sales of any equity securities of the issuer, and requires him to turn over to the company any profit derived from a purchase and sale of such securities within a six-month period.

§ 13. Periodic Disclosure Requirements

One principal thrust of the Securities Exchange Act of 1934 was to assure the public availability of adequate information about companies with publicly-traded stocks. As amended in 1964, the Act's disclosure requirements apply not only to companies with securities listed on national securities exchanges, but also to all companies with more than 500 shareholders and more than $1,000,000 of assets. SEA § 12(a), (g). Certain special types of issuers are exempted, including investment companies, § 12(g)(2)(B), and insurance companies if they are subject to comparable state requirements, § 12(g)(2)(G). Banks are subject to the requirements, but administration and enforcement with respect to them are vested in the federal banking agencies rather than the SEC. § 12(i). As of December 31, 1973, more than 10,000 companies were subject to 1934 Act disclosure requirements, of which about 3,000 had securities listed on exchanges and about 7,000 had securities traded solely in the over-the-counter market.

The specific requirements for disclosure of information about the issuing company are found in SEA §§ 12, 13, and 14. § 12 requires the filing of a detailed statement about the company when it first registers under the 1934 Act, and § 13 requires a registered company to file with the SEC "such annual reports * * * and such quarterly reports   *   *   *   as the Commission may prescribe."

In October 1970, the Commission adopted revisions of its forms for registration and reporting under SEA §§ 12 and 13. Form 10, the general form for initial registration of a class of securities under § 12, was revised to make its disclosures correspond more closely to those required in a 1933 Act registration statement or a proxy statement under § 14 of the 1934 Act. SEA Rel. 8996. Form 10–K, the general form of annual report for companies registered under the 1934 Act, was revised "to provide on an annual basis information which, together with that contained in the proxy or information statement sent to security holders, will furnish a reasonably complete and up-to-date statement of the business and operations of the registrant." SEA Rel. 9000. A new form 10–Q was adopted, under which registered companies must file quarterly reports containing summarized financial information for each of the first three quarters of their fiscal years. SEA Rel. 9004. Form 10–Q was substantially amended in 1977, to increase the amount of information reporting companies must furnish on a quarterly basis. SEA Rel. 13156.

SEA § 18 makes a company liable in damages to any person who buys or sells its securities in reliance on a misleading statement contained in any application, report or other document that the company has filed with the Commission under that Act. See Heit v. Weitzen, 402 F.2d 909 (2d Cir. 1968).

§ 14. Proxy Solicitation

SEA § 14 makes it unlawful for a company registered under SEA § 12 to solicit proxies from its shareholders "in contravention of such rules and regulations as the Commission may prescribe as necessary or appropriate in the public interest or for the protection of investors." In 1964, the reach of § 14 was broadened by the addition of § 14(c), under which a company, even if it does not solicit proxies from its shareholders in connection with a meeting, must furnish them with information "substantially equivalent" to that which would be required if it did solicit proxies. Under § 14(f), added in 1968, a corporation must also make disclosures to shareholders when a majority of its board of directors is replaced by action of the directors, without a shareholders' meeting, in connection with the transfer of a controlling stock interest.

Disclosure. Under this authority, the Commission has promulgated detailed regulations prescribing the form of proxy and the information to be furnished to shareholders. Prior to every meeting of its security holders, a registered company must furnish each of them with a "proxy statement" containing the information specified in SEA Schedule 14A, together with a form of proxy on which the security holder can indicate his approval or disapproval of each proposal expected to be presented at the meeting. SEA Rules 14a–3, 4. Where securities are registered in the names of brokers, banks or nominees, the company must inquire as to the beneficial ownership of the securities, furnish sufficient copies of the proxy statement for distribution to all of the beneficial owners, and pay the reasonable expenses of such distribution. SEA Rule 14a–3(d).

Preliminary copies of the proxy statement and form of proxy must be filed with the SEC at least 10 days before they are sent to security holders, and definitive copies must be filed at the time of mailing. Rule 14a–6. Although the proxy statement does not have to become "effective" in the same manner as a 1933 Act registration statement (see § 8 *supra*), the SEC will often comment on, and insist on changes in, the proxy statement before it is mailed.

When the proxies are being solicited for use at an annual meeting for election of directors, the proxy statement must be accompanied by an annual report containing comparative financial statements for the last two fiscal years and other specified information. SEA Rules 14a–3, 14c–3. The impact of this requirement was substantially increased in 1974 when the SEC amended its rules to require that registered companies include in their annual reports to shareholders substantial portions of the financial and business information included in their annual reports to the SEC. SEA Rel. 11079.

Proxy Contests. The SEC proxy rules apply to all solicitations of proxies, consents or authorizations from security holders, by the management or anyone else, subject to exceptions specified in SEA Rule 14a–2. When there is a contest with respect to election or removal of directors, Rule 14a–11 imposes special procedural requirements, and calls for the filing with the Commission of additional information specified in Schedule 14B.

Shareholder Proposals. Under SEA Rule 14a–8, if any security holder of a registered company gives timely notice to the management of his intention to present a proposal for action at a forthcoming meeting, the management must include the proposal in its proxy statement and afford security holders an opportunity to vote for or against it in the management's proxy. In addition, if the management opposes the proposal, it must include in its proxy material a statement by the security holder, not more than 200 words in length, in support of his proposal.

This rule has been extensively utilized by proponents of "shareholder democracy," to require inclusion of proposals relating to management compensation, conduct of annual meetings, shareholder voting rights, and similar matters. It has also been utilized by persons opposed to the Vietnam war, discrimination, pollution, and other evils, to attempt to force changes in company policies that affect those matters.

Since management generally resists the inclusion of shareholder proposals, the provisions of the rule specifying the kinds of proposals that can be omitted have been the subject of constant controversy and frequent change. As presently in effect, Rule 14a–8(c) permits management to exclude a proposal if, among other things, it

(1) is, under the governing state law, not a proper subject for action by security holders;

(2) relates to a personal claim or grievance;

(3) is not significantly related to the company's business or is beyond the company's power to effectuate;

(4) relates to the conduct of the company's ordinary business operations;

(5) relates to elections to office (security holders may not use the rule to nominate candidates for the board of directors); or

(6) is substantially similar to a proposal previously submitted during the past five years, which received affirmative votes from less than a specified percentage of the shares voted.

In case of a dispute between management and a shareholder as to whether a particular proposal may be excluded from the proxy statement, the decision in the first instance is for the SEC. The Commission initially took the position that its refusal to direct a company to include a proposal is not an "order" subject to judicial review under SEA § 25, but one court disagreed. Medical Committee v. SEC, 432 F.2d 659 (D.C. Cir. 1970), vacated as moot, 404 U.S. 403 (1972). However, the Commission subsequently discovered that it could avoid judicial review by delegating to its staff the power to decide individual cases, and declining to review the staff decision. Kixmiller v. SEC, 492 F.2d 641 (D.C. Cir. 1974).

(a) Civil Liability

A company which distributes a misleading proxy statement to its shareholders may incur liability under SEA § 18 to any person who purchases or sells its securities in reliance on the misleading statement. See § 13 *supra*. In addition, SEA Rule 14a–9 makes it unlawful to solicit proxies by means of any proxy statement or other communication "containing any statement which * * * is false or misleading with respect to any material fact, or which omits to state any material fact necessary in order to make the statement therein not false or misleading * * *." While the 1934 Act does not explicitly create any civil liability for a violation of

§ 14 or the SEC's rules under it, the question arose whether a shareholder, who alleged that the votes to approve a merger or other transaction were obtained by means of a misleading proxy statement, had a right of action for damages or other relief. In J. I. Case Co. v. Borak, 377 U.S. 426 (1964), the Supreme Court held that a shareholder had such an implied right of action under SEA § 14, by virtue of the language of § 27, which grants federal district courts jurisdiction of all actions "to enforce any liability or duty created by" the Act. The recognition of this implied private right of action, however, has created a number of difficult questions of interpretation and implementation.

Causation. One question is what showing the plaintiff must make that shareholder approval of the transaction was a result of the misstatement, particularly where a substantial portion of the shares were held by "insiders" who had full knowledge of the true facts. In Mills v. Electric Auto-Lite Co., 396 U.S. 375 (1970), the Supreme Court held that, where some votes of "outside" shareholders were necessary for approval, plaintiff was only required to show that the misstatement or omission was "material", not that it actually had a decisive effect on the voting.

A more difficult question arises if the "insiders" have enough shares to approve the transaction without the votes of any of the "outside" shareholders. However, even in that situation, at least one court of appeals has held that the plaintiff should still be entitled to sue, on the ground that the "broad remedial purposes" of the proxy rules to ensure "fair corporate suffrage" made it inappropriate to apply a strict causation rule. Schlick v. Penn-Dixie Cement Corp., 507 F.2d 374 (2d Cir. 1974); see also Swanson v. American Consumer Industries, 475 F.2d 516 (7th Cir. 1973).

Materiality. In *Mills,* Justice Harlan stated the test for materiality of a misstatement or omission in a proxy statement as whether "it *might* have been considered important by a reasonable shareholder." However, in TSC Industries v. Northway, 426 U.S. 438 (1976), the Supreme Court adopted a stricter standard, holding that "an omitted fact is material if there is *a substantial likelihood* that a reasonable shareholder would consider it important in deciding how to vote * * *. Put another way, there must be a substantial likelihood that the disclosure of the omitted fact would have been viewed by the reasonable invester as having significantly altered the 'total mix' of information made available."

Culpability. In Gerstle v. Gamble-Skogmo, 478 F.2d 1281 (2d Cir. 1973), the court held that in an action under Rule 14a–9, unlike an action under SEA Rule 10b–5 (see § 20(b) *infra*), negligence in the preparation of the proxy statement would be sufficient to warrant recovery, and that no evil motive or reckless disregard of the facts need be shown.

Relief.   In appropriate cases, a court may grant equitable relief, such as ordering a new election of directors when proxies for the election of the incumbents were procured by a misleading proxy statement.   Gladwin v. Medfield Corp., 540 F.2d 1266 (5th Cir. 1976).   However, plaintiff's showing of a violation does not automatically entitle him to equitable relief.   In *Mills,* the court said that a merger should not be set aside unless such action would be in the best interest of all the shareholders, and plaintiff in that case was remitted to his damage remedy.

Computation of damages in a merger situation can involve difficult questions, such as the appropriate value of the acquired company, as in *Swanson,* or the acquiring company's liability for all profits resulting from the merger, as in *Gerstle.* In *Mills* itself, the courts ultimately held that since the terms of the merger were not unfair, plaintiff was not entitled to any damages, even though there had been a material omission from the proxy statement.   Mills v. Electric Auto-Lite Co., 552 F.2d 1239 (7th Cir. 1977).

Remedies Under 1933 Act.   As a result of the adoption of SA Rule 145 (see § 10(d) *supra*), most proxy statements used in connection with mergers, reclassifications and sales of assets are now also 1933 Act registration statements, so that the civil liability provisions of § 11 of that Act provide an alternative avenue of relief for aggrieved shareholders of acquired companies who can establish material misstatements or omissions in the proxy statement.

§ 15. Takeover Bids and Tender Offers

During the "conglomerate" craze of the 1960s, aggressively-managed corporations, in increasing numbers, embarked on compaigns to acquire controlling stock interests in other publicly-held corporations. They might acquire the stock for cash, or by issuing their own securities in exchange, or some combination of the two. They might acquire stock in private transactions, by purchases through brokers in the open market, or by making a public offer to the shareholders of the target company to tender their shares, either for a fixed cash price or for a package of securities of the offering corporation. These "takeover bids" or "tender offers" were often bitterly opposed by the management of the target corporation, and the contests featured flamboyant public claims and charges on both sides, efforts to manipulate the market, and confusing and coercive approaches to the shareholders of the target corporation.

Where the takeover bid involved a public offer of securities of the aggressor corporation in exchange for shares of the target corporation, the securities of course had to be registered under the Securities Act of 1933 and a prospectus delivered to the shareholders being solicited. In the case of a cash tender offer, however, there was no requirement for the filing of any solicitation material with the SEC.

The "Williams Act," passed in 1968, was designed to give the SEC and the courts power to deal with these problems. It added several new provisions to the 1934 Act. Those directly applicable to takeover bids are § 13(d) and §§ 14(d) and (e).

Filing of Statement. Under SEA § 13(d), any person (or "group") that becomes the owner of more than 5% of any class of securities registered under SEA § 12 must file with the issuer of the securities, and with the Commission, within 10 days, a statement setting forth (a) the background of such person, (b) the source of the funds used for the acquisition, (c) the purpose of the acquisition, (d) the number of shares owned, and (e) any relevant contracts, arrangements or understandings. An issuer has an implied private right of action against a person who fails to file the report, but is not entitled to an injunction restraining the voting of the securities or acquisition of additional securities without showing "irreparable harm and other usual prerequisites for injunctive relief." Rondeau v. Mosinee Paper Corp., 422 U.S. 49 (1975).

One difficult question under § 13(d) arises where a number of shareholders of a company, owning in the aggregate more than 5% of its shares, agree to act together for the purpose of affecting the control of the company, but do not acquire any additional shares. The courts have split as to whether the agreement to act together constitutes an "acquisition" by the "group", triggering the filing requirement. Compare GAF Corp. v. Milstein, 453 F.2d 709 (2d Cir. 1971), with Bath Industries v. Blot, 427 F.2d 97 (7th Cir. 1970).

Tender Offer Procedures. Under SEA § 14(d), no person may make a tender offer which would result in his owning more than 5% of a class of securities registered under § 12 unless he has filed with the Commission, and furnishes to each offeree, a statement containing certain of the information required under § 13(d). See Rule 14d–1(d). § 14(d) also imposes certain substantive restrictions on the terms of an offer, with respect to such matters as right of withdrawal, pro rata acceptance, and extensions and variations of the offer.

The term "tender offer" is not defined in the Act. It has been held not to encompass purchases in the open market, whether or not made for purposes of obtaining control. Water & Wall Assoc. v. American Consumer Industries, CCH ¶ 93,943 (D.N.J.1973). However, it has been held to include "any public invitation to a corporation's shareholders to purchase their stock," even though it is not a "hostile bid opposed by incumbent management." Smallwood v. Pearl Brewing Co., 489 F.2d 579 (5th Cir. 1974).

Misstatements in Tender Offers.   SEA § 14(e) makes it unlawful for any person to misstate or omit a material fact, or engage in any fraudulent, deceptive or manipulative acts or practices, in connection with a tender offer.   There is no express private right of action for a violation of this prohibition.   However, in Electronic Specialty Co. v. International Controls Corp., 409 F.2d 937 (2d Cir. 1969), the court held that the target corporation had standing to seek an injunction against an aggressor which had made misleading statements in the course of a tender offer.   On the other hand, the Supreme Court held in Piper v. Chris-Craft Industries, 97 S.Ct. 926 (1977), that a defeated tender offeror had no standing to sue for damages allegedly resulting from misleading statements made by its opponents in the struggle for control.   While the Court did not pass on the standing of a tender offeror to seek equitable relief, or the standing of the target corporation, it indicated that it might imply a private right of action under § 14(e) only where it would benefit the shareholders of the target corporation, the group which Congress intended to protect.

To the extent that private rights of action are recognized under § 14(e), they can give rise to the same questions of causation, culpability and relief that arise in merger proxy litigation (see § 14(a) *supra*). In Piper v. Chris-Craft, *supra,* the court of appeals had held (a) that the tender offeror could recover if it could show that the target company made material misstatements to its shareholders that affected the offeror's ability to acquire a majority of the shares, (b) that the defendants could be held civilly liable if they knew their statement to be untrue or "failed or refused to ascertain the facts" when the facts were available to them, and (c) that the plaintiff was entitled to damages measured by the difference between the price which it actually paid for the shares it acquired and the value they had as a minority interest. See 480 F.2d 341 (2d Cir. 1973); 516 F.2d 172 (2d Cir. 1975). In view of its disposition of the case, the Supreme Court did not pass on these issues; however, the concurring and dissenting opinions indicate that the Court would have taken a more restrictive view than the court of appeals.

§ 16. Liability for "Short-Swing" Profits

The last of the provisions applicable to companies which have securities registered under SEA § 12 is SEA § 16, which is designed to discourage corporate "insiders" from taking advantage of

their access to information by engaging in short-term trading in the corporation's securities. §
16(a) requires every person who beneficially owns, directly or indirectly, more than 10% of a class of equity securities registered under SEA §
12, and every officer and director of every company that has a class of equity securities registered under that section, to file a report with the SEC (a) at the time he acquires such status and (b) at the end of any month in which he acquires or disposes of any equity securities of that company. "For the purpose of preventing the unfair use of information which may have been obtained by" any such officer, director or 10% shareholder, § 16(b) permits the company, or any security holder suing on its behalf, to recover any "profit" realized by any person from any purchase and sale, or sale and purchase, of any equity security of the company within a period of less than six months.

There are several important things to note about § 16. First, although its purpose is to prevent unfair use of inside information, it does not reach all instances of such use, but only specified combinations of transactions by specified classes of people. But where the statute does apply, it is not necessary to show that the defendant actually took advantage of, or had access to, inside information. Smolowe v. Delendo Corp., 136 F.2d 231 (2d Cir. 1943). In interpreting the specific words such as "purchase", "sale" and "beneficial owner," however, most courts have followed the "pragmatic" approach of attempting to determine whether the particular transaction presented the possibilities for the type of abuse with which Congress was concerned. See Kern County Land Co. v. Occidental Petroleum Corp., 411 U.S. 582, 594 n. 26 (1973).

Second, while the SEC has statutory power under § 16(b) to exempt by rule transactions which it finds to be "not comprehended within the purpose of [that] subsection," see Greene v. Dietz, 247 F.2d 689 (2d Cir. 1957), the SEC has no enforcement powers under § 16. Liability can be asserted only in a suit brought by the issuer or a security holder suing on its behalf. Since corporate management will seldom be inclined to sue its own members, and since the financial benefit to any individual security holder bringing suit on the issuer's behalf will ordinarily be infinitesimal, the principal incentive to enforcement of the section is the fee which the court awards to the attorney for the plaintiff out of the profits recovered by the company. While the principal financial interest in a § 16(b) suit is that of the attorney, rather than the "client", the courts have refused to bar such actions on the basis of improper motivation or unprofessional conduct, reasoning that Congress must have intended to accept such conduct as the price of effective enforcement of that particular type of provision. See Magida v. Continental Can Co., 176 F.Supp. 781 (S.D.N.Y.1956).

"Profit Realized".   There is a "profit" for § 16(b) purposes whenever there is a purchase that can be matched against a sale at a higher price that is made less than six months after, or before, the purchase.   Securities are fungible for § 16(b) purposes; there is no need to trace certificates. Smolowe v. Delendo Corp., *supra*.   Indeed, sales of common stock can be matched against purchases of debentures convertible into common stock to produce a "profit".   Chemical Fund v. Xerox Corp., 377 F.2d 107 (2d Cir. 1967).   Also, there is no provision for offsetting "losses" against "profits".   Where a defendant has engaged in a series of transactions at varying prices, the "profit" recoverable by the company is determined by matching the highest-price sales against the lowest-price purchases, so that he may be held liable for "profits" even where he has suffered an overall trading loss during the six-month period involved.   Chemical Fund v. Xerox Corp., *supra*.

"Director" or "Officer".   The terms "director" and "officer" include persons performing the functions usually associated with those positions. A purchase or sale made by a person while he is a director or officer can be matched against a sale or purchase made within six months but be-

fore he assumed that position or after he resigned. See SEA Rule 16a–1(d), (e); Adler v. Klawans, 267 F.2d 840 (2d Cir. 1959); Feder v. Martin Marietta Corp., 406 F.2d 260 (2d Cir. 1969). However, a purchase and sale both made within the six-month period following resignation as a director are not covered. Levy v. Seaton, 358 F.Supp. 1 (S.D.N.Y.1973).

A partnership or corporation that is found to have "deputized" one of its members or officers to serve as a director of another company will itself be liable as a "director" under § 16(b) for profits made on its own trades. Blau v. Lehman, 368 U.S. 403 (1962); Feder v. Martin Marietta Corp., *supra*. However, "deputization" is a question of fact, and where a partner is found not to have been representing the partnership on the board of the company, § 16(b) liability will attach only to his pro rata share of profits on the partnership's trading activities. Blau v. Lehman, *supra*.

Transactions by directors or officers may or may not be matched against transactions by their spouses or other family members, depending on whether their investment activities are "directed toward their common prosperity." Compare Whiting v. Dow Chemical Co., 523 F.2d 680 (2d Cir. 1975) with Blau v. Potter, CCH ¶ 94,115 (S. D.N.Y.1973).

"10% Shareholder".   To be liable as a beneficial owner, a person must own more than 10% of a class of *registered equity securities*.   Ownership of more than 10% of the common stock, or of a registered preferred stock (i. e. a class held by more than 500 persons, see SEA § 12(g)), will of course suffice.   However, ownership of more than 10% of a class of convertible debentures (which are considered "equity securities" under § 3(a)(11) only because they are convertible into common stock) does not make the holder liable under § 16(b) unless the common stock into which his debentures are convertible, plus any other common stock he owns, would amount to more than 10% of the common stock outstanding. Chemical Fund v. Xerox Corp., *supra*; see Rule 16a–2(b).

In contrast to the situation with respect to directors and officers, § 16(b) specifically provides that a beneficial owner can be held liable only if he was a 10% shareholder at the time of both the purchase and the sale.   The Supreme Court has held that the purchase which makes a person a 10% shareholder cannot be matched against a subsequent sale to create liability.   Foremost-McKesson v. Provident Securities Co., 423 U.S. 232 (1976).   It has also held that a holder of more than 10% who first sells enough to bring his holdings down to 9.9%, and then sells the remainder, cannot be held liable for the profit on the second transaction, even if the two sales were parts of a single prearranged plan. Reliance Electric Co. v. Emerson Electric Co., 404 U.S. 418 (1972).

"Purchase" and "Sale". In addition to normal cash transactions, the acquisition of an option to buy or sell securities at a fixed price will constitute a "purchase" or "sale". Giving another person an option to buy, however, will not constitute a "sale" unless the size of the payment for the option or other factors indicate that it was intended to be a completed sale. Compare Kern County Land Co. v. Occidental Petroleum Corp., *supra,* with Bershad v. McDonough, 428 F.2d 693 (7th Cir. 1970).

Conversion of a convertible security into common stock does not normally constitute a "sale" of the former or a "purchase" of the latter. Blau v. Lamb, 363 F.2d 507 (2d Cir. 1966). Surrender of securities of one company for securities of another company in a statutory merger may constitute a "sale" and "purchase" if the defendant had power to put through the merger and there was a possibility for use of inside information. Newmark v. RKO General, 425 F.2d 348 (2d Cir. 1970). However, where the defendant is a "forced seller" (e. g., a defeated tender offeror which is forced to exchange its shares because it has insufficient votes to prevent the merger from going through), its disposition is not considered a "sale" for § 16(b) purposes. Kern County Land Co. v. Occidental Petroleum Corp., *supra*. Furthermore, if it subsequently disposes of its shares in the surviving company at a "profit" within six months from the time it purchased its shares of the acquired company, the two transactions cannot be matched under § 16(b) since they did not involve securities of the same "issuer". American Standard v. Crane Co., 510 F.2d 1043 (2d Cir. 1974).

IV. ANTIFRAUD PROVISIONS

Most of the preceding sections of this book have dealt with specific, and often very elaborate, provisions of law or regulations designed to deal with particular kinds of transactions or practices. However, some of the most important developments in federal securities law have grown out of the "antifraud" provisions found in those laws— generalized prohibitions against "fraud or deceit" or "manipulative or deceptive devices or contrivances."

Provisions of this type are found in SA § 17(a), SEA §§ 10(b), 14(e) and 15(c)(1), and IAA § 206. Because SEA § 10(b) has the broadest jurisdictional reach, it is the provision most frequently invoked, but the doctrines developed under it are also applicable to the other sections.

§ 17. Market Manipulation

One of the most serious abuses in the securities markets on which Senate investigators focused, in the hearings which led to enactment of the 1934 Act, was the operation of "pools" which ran up the prices of securities on an exchange by series of well-timed transactions, effected solely for the purpose of "manipulating" the market price of the security, then unloaded their holdings on the public just before the price dropped. Accordingly, SEA §§ 9 and 10(a) prohibit a variety of manipulative activities with respect to exchange-listed securities, and § 10(b) contains a catch-all provision permitting the SEC to prohibit by rule any "manipulative or deceptive device or contrivance" with respect to any security.

By and large, these provisions have been effective in preventing a recurrence of the widespread manipulation on exchanges which flourished in the 1920's. The present focus of concern, at least with respect to stocks listed on the New York Stock Exchange, is the extent to which large transactions by "institutional investors", such as pension funds, mutual funds and insurance companies, produce undesirable fluctuations and distortions in the market price of particular securities. This problem, however, results from changes in investment patterns and other economic factors, rather than from the type of deliberate fraud with which the draftsmen of the 1934 Act were concerned.

There are several areas in which there have been continuing problems in drawing the line between manipulative activity and legitimate transactions. One is the extent to which securities dealers and others participating in a public offering or "distribution" of securities may simultaneously bid for or purchase the same security. Another is the extent to which corporations may influence the price of their own shares by purchasing them in the open market. A third is the activities of the participants in contested takeover bids.

(a) Distributions

The success of a public offering of securities may depend in large measure on whether the market price of the security goes up or down during the period of the distribution. Accordingly, there is a strong incentive for those participating in the distribution to maintain the market price at a high level during that period. On the other hand, the injection of a large new block of securities into the trading market may exert a temporary depressing influence on the market price and make it impossible for the underwriters to market the new shares at a price near the previously prevailing market price. The SEC therefore faced the question whether to permit the underwriters to "stabilize" the price—i. e., to place a bid for the securities in the market at or near the public offering price, and to purchase (for resale) shares coming into the market that might otherwise cause the market price to drop.

As early as 1936, the Commission decided that "certain stabilizing operations" were not within the Act's prohibitions against manipulation, and permitted underwriters to support, within limits, the price of the security being distributed. Since 1939, SA Rule 426 has required that every prospectus set forth the possibility of underwriters' stabilizing purchases, and SEA Rule 17a–2 has required detailed reports to the SEC by the underwriters when they do in fact stabilize.

Precise guidelines as to when, and at what price, underwriters may enter stabilizing bids were finally laid down in 1955 with the adoption of SEA Rules 10b–6, –7 and –8. Rule 10b–6 makes it unlawful for any underwriter or other person participating in a "distribution" to bid for or purchase any units of the security being distributed, with certain specified exceptions. Rule 10b–7 specifies the terms on which "stabilizing" bids may be made or changed, and Rule 10b–8 specifies the transactions in which "standby underwriters" may engage when a company is offering securities to its existing shareholders in a "rights offering."

Rules 10b–6 and –7 are tailored to the normal firm-commitment underwriting in which a fixed number of shares are offered at one time at a fixed price. There are serious difficulties in applying them to unorganized "distributions" (as, for example, when a group of shareholders plan to make sales from time to time at prevailing prices through brokers or dealers in the exchange or over-the-counter markets). No stabilizing is permitted under Rule 10b–7 in such offerings "at the market", but there are problems in determining what constitutes a "distribution" for Rule 10b–6 purposes, and who should be deemed to be "participating" in it. See Hazel Bishop, 40 S.E.C. 718 (1961); Jaffee & Co., 44 S.E.C. 285 (1970); Collins Securities, SEA Rel. 11766 (1975).

"Hot Issues." The opposite side of the "stabilizing" problem is presented by the "hot issue"— a new issue which jumps to a substantial premium over the offering price as soon as secondary trading commences. This phenomenon typically occurs during periods of speculative frenzy, when almost any issue of a small, unknown company will jump to an immediate premium because of large demand and a small supply of stock. The efforts of the SEC and the NASD have been concentrated on assuring that the underwriters do not artificially stimulate demand or restrict the supply of stock, and that they do not profit by "free riding," i. e. withholding some of the stock from the public during the initial offering in expectation of selling it at a higher price in the secondary market.

(b) Corporate Repurchases

Corporations may purchase their own shares in the open market (or cause such shares to be purchased for employee pension or profit-sharing plans). Such purchases may have the effect (and sometimes the purpose) of raising the market price of the company's stock above the level that would otherwise prevail. They may raise problems even when the company is not technically engaged in a distribution and therefore not subject to the prohibitions of Rule 10b–6.

Between 1961 and 1966, Georgia-Pacific Corp. acquired a number of other companies in exchange for its own stock, with the total number of shares to be delivered depending on whether G–P stock reached a specified price level within a certain period. The SEC brought an injunction action against G–P, charging that, during that period, G–P had purchased 23,000 shares of its own stock for its employee bonus plan, and that "such purchases were intentionally effected in a manner which would and did, directly and indirectly cause the last sale price of G–P common stock on the NYSE to rise in order that G–P's obligation to issue additional shares * * * would be avoided or reduced". At the SEC's request, the court issued an injunction restraining G–P from repurchasing any shares while the terms of an acquisition or exchange offer were being determined, or from repurchasing shares at any time (a) through orders placed with more than one broker, (b) at the opening or close of the market, (c) at a price above the last sale or current bid price, or (d) in excess of 10% of the current weekly trading volume or 15% of the current daily trading volume. SEC v. Georgia-Pacific Corp., CCH ¶ ¶ 91,680, 91,692 (S.D.N.Y.1966).

In 1968, as part of the "Williams Act" to regulate take-over bids and tender offers, Congress enacted SEA § 13(e), specifically authorizing the SEC to regulate corporate repurchases of their own securities, for the purpose of preventing "fraudulent, deceptive or manipulative acts or practices." Pursuant to this authority, the Commission has proposed SEA Rule 13e–2, which would impose on all registered companies restrictions roughly comparable to those imposed on Georgia-Pacific by the 1966 injunction. See SEA Rels. 8930 (1970), 10359 (1973). While the rule has not been formally adopted, it is thought to be widely followed in practice.

(c) Contested Takeover Bids

In the course of a contest for control of a target company (see § 15 *supra*) one contestant may make purchases of stock of the target company for the purpose of affecting its market price or in a way which violates the specific prohibitions of SEA Rules 10b–6 and 10b–13. The courts have held, however, that the opposing contestant, against whom such practices are directed, has no standing to sue for damages resulting from the violation. Piper v. Chris-Craft Industries, 97 S. Ct. 926 (1977) (technical violation of Rule 10b–6); Crane Co. v. American-Standard, CCH ¶ 96,-160 (S.D.N.Y.1977) (deliberate manipulation in violation of § 9).

§ 18. The Jurisprudence of Rule 10b–5

SEA § 10(b) is a catch-all provision, designed to deal with abuses that escaped the specific prohibitions of §§ 9 and 10(a). It makes it unlawful for any person to use the mails or facilities of interstate commerce:

> "To use or employ, in connection with the purchase or sale of any security * * * any manipulative or deceptive device or contrivance in contravention of such rules and regulations as the Commission may prescribe as necessary or appropriate in the public interest or for the protection of investors."

Note that § 10(b) by its terms does not make anything unlawful unless the Commission has adopted a rule prohibiting it.

In 1942, the Commission was presented with a situation in which the president of a company was buying shares from the existing shareholders at a low price by misrepresenting the company's financial condition. While SA § 17(a) prohibited fraud and misstatements in the *sale* of securities, there was no comparable provision prohibiting such practices in connection with the *purchase* of securities. The SEC's Assistant Solicitor accordingly lifted the operative language out of § 17(a), made the necessary modifications, added the words "in connection with the purchase or sale of any security," and presented the product to the Commission as SEA Rule 10b–5. It was unanimously approved without discussion. Remarks of Milton Freeman, 22 Bus.Lawyer 922 (1967).

As adopted (and it has not been amended), Rule 10b–5 states:

"It shall be unlawful for any person, directly or indirectly, by the use of any means or instrumentality of interstate commerce, or of the mails, or of any facility of any national securities exchange,

"(1) to employ any device, scheme, or artifice to defraud,

"(2) to make any untrue statement of a material fact or to omit to state a material fact necessary in order to make the statements made, in the light of circumstances under which they were made, not misleading, or

"(3) to engage in any act, practice, or course of business which operates or would operate as a fraud or deceit upon any person,

in connection with the purchase or sale of any security." In the 35 years since its adoption, this

[*116*]

simple rule has been invoked in countless SEC and private proceedings, and applied to almost every conceivable kind of situation. It has spawned a formidable outpouring of legal scholarship, including two complete books and innumerable law review articles. But before examining systematically this body of jurisprudence of SEA Rule 10b–5, it is necessary to have in mind certain basic features of the rule:

1. It applies to any purchase or sale by any person of any security. There are no exemptions. It applies to securities which are registered under the 1934 Act, or which are not so registered. It applies to publicly-held companies, to closely-held companies, to any kind of entity which issues something that can be called a "security." It even applies to "exempted securities", as defined in SEA § 3(a)(12), (including federal, state and local government securities) which are specifically exempted from certain other provisions of the Act. Because of this broad scope, the rule may be invoked in many situations in which alternative remedies are made available (or are not made available) by applicable provisions of federal securities laws or state securities or corporation laws. Thus there is often a question as to the extent to which Rule 10b–5 should be available to by-pass procedural or substantive restrictions in other laws.

2. It is an "antifraud" provision. It was adopted by the SEC under authority of a section

designed to prohibit "any manipulative or deceptive device or contrivance," and two of its three operative clauses are based on the concept of "fraud" or "deceit" (the fact that clause (2) is worded in terms of "untrue statements or omissions" rather than "fraud" raises some problems to be discussed below). While the courts have applied it in some situations where there was no showing of willful misconduct, they have been uncomfortable about extending it too far, particularly in private actions for damages.

3. It is worded as a prohibition; there are no express provisions anywhere in the securities laws prescribing any civil liability for its violation. However, as far back as 1946, the courts took the position that they would follow the normal tort rule that a person who violates a legislative enactment is liable in damages if he invades an interest of another person that the legislation was intended to protect. Kardon v. National Gypsum Co., 69 F.Supp. 512 (E.D.Pa.1946).

In the 1960's and early 1970's, many federal appellate courts and district courts developed expansive interpretations of Rule 10b–5 (and other antifraud provisions of the securities laws). They applied it to impose liability for negligent as well as deliberate misrepresentations, for breaches of fiduciary duty by corporate management, and for failure by directors, underwriters, accountants and lawyers to prevent wrongdoing by others. In private actions for damages, the courts were willing to imply a private right of action in anyone whose losses were even remotely connected with the alleged wrongdoing, or even in someone who had suffered no loss if his suit would help to encourage compliance with the law. The Supreme Court aided and abetted this development, giving an expansive reading to the terms "fraud" and "purchase or sale" and to the "connection" that had to be found between them. SEC v. Capital Gains Research Bureau, 375 U.S. 180 (1963) ("fraud"); Affiliated Ute Citizens v. U. S., 406 U.S. 128 (1972) ("fraud"); SEC v. National Securities, 393 U.S. 453 (1969) ("purchase or sale"); Sup't of Insurance v. Bankers Life & Casualty Co., 404 U.S. 6 (1971) ("in connection with").

Starting in 1975, a new conservative majority on the Supreme Court has sharply reversed this trend, in a series of decisions giving a narrow reading to the terms of Rule 10b–5 and other antifraud provisions, and limiting the situations in which a private right of action will be implied. On the substantive side, it has held that the term "fraud" does not include overreaching by a controlling shareholder unless accompanied by actual deception, and that no person can be held liable for damages under Rule 10b–5 unless he can be shown to have acted with *scienter*. Santa Fe Industries v. Green, 97 S.Ct. 1292 (1977); Ernst &

Ernst v. Hochfelder, 425 U.S. 185 (1976). With respect to private rights of action, it has held that only a "purchaser" or "seller" can sue under Rule 10b–5, and that strict criteria will be applied in determining whether any person should have an implied right to sue under any of the antifraud provisions. Blue Chip Stamps v. Manor Drug Stores, 421 U.S. 723 (1975); Piper v. Chris-Craft Industries, 97 S.Ct. 926 (1977).

The tone of these recent Supreme Court decisions is even more important than their actual holdings. They cast doubt on the continued vitality of many of the expansive decisions of the preceding 15 years, even those that have not been specifically overruled. This fact should be kept in mind in evaluating the discussion in the following four sections, which summarize the current law in the principal categories of transactions to which Rule 10b–5 has been applied.

§ 19. Insider Trading

One of the most important applications of Rule 10b–5 is its use as a sanction against "insider trading"—purchases or sales by persons who have access to information which is not available to those with whom they deal or to traders generally.

Early applications of the rule focused on the situation with which it was specifically designed to deal—purchases in direct transactions by the corporation or its officers without disclosure of material favorable information about the company's affairs. Ward La France Truck Corp., 13 S. E.C. 373 (1943); Speed v. Transamerica Corp., 99 F.Supp. 808 (D.Del.1951). In this context, it was available to supplement state common law, which in most states did not afford a remedy to the aggrieved seller in this situation in the absence of affirmative misstatements or "special circumstances."

In a series of administrative decisions and injunctive proceedings, commencing in 1961, the SEC greatly broadened the applicability of Rule 10b–5 as a general prohibition against any trading on "inside information" in anonymous stock exchange transactions as well as in face-to-face dealings. The three most significant decisions were Cady, Roberts & Co., 40 S.E.C. 907 (1961), SEC v. Texas Gulf Sulphur Co., 401 F.2d 833 (2d Cir. 1968), and Investors Management Co., 44 S.E.C. 633 (1971).

(a) Elements of the Violation

In *Cady Roberts,* a partner in a brokerage firm received a message from a director of Curtiss-Wright that the board of directors had just voted to cut the dividend. He immediately placed orders to sell Curtiss-Wright stock for some of his customers, and the sales were made before the news of the dividend cut was generally disseminated.   In *Texas Gulf Sulphur,* officers and employees of the company made substantial purchases of the company's stock after learning that exploratory drilling on one of the company's properties showed promise of an extraordinary ore discovery (although the drilling had not gone far enough to establish whether there was a commercially mineable body of ore).   In *Investors Management,* an aircraft manufacturer disclosed to a broker-dealer, which was acting as principal underwriter for a proposed debenture issue, that its earnings for the current year would be substantially less than it had previously forecast publicly.   The broker-dealer's underwriting department passed the information to members of its sales department, who in turn passed it to representatives of major institutional clients.   The institutions sold large amounts of stock before the revised earnings estimate became public.

In all three cases, the persons who effected the transactions (or who passed information to those persons) were held to have violated Rule 10b–5. The scope of the prohibition, as it emerges from these decisions, seems roughly as follows:

Which Clause is Violated?   The opinions have not been terribly clear as to which clause of the rule prohibits insider trading.   Since all three cases involved total nondisclosure, they presumably did not violate clause (2), which requires some "statement."   In *Cady Roberts,* the Commission said that the broker's conduct "at least violated clause (3) as a practice which operated as a fraud or deceit upon the purchasers" and that there was therefore no need to decide the scope of clauses (1) and (2). Subsequent decisions have not significantly clarified this question.

To Whom is the Duty Owed? If clause (3) is violated, is it because of a "fraud or deceit" on the company or on persons on the other side of the market? In *Cady Roberts,* the Commission indicated that there were elements of both: "The obligation rests on two principal elements; first, the existence of a relationship giving access, directly or indirectly, to information intended to be available only for a corporate purpose and not for the personal benefit of anyone, and second, the inherent unfairness involved where a party takes advantage of such information knowing it is unavailable to those with whom he is dealing." However, subsequent decisions have focused on the second element and, as noted below, the rule may apply to information that would affect the price of the company's stock, even if it did not originate from the company.

The Commission in *Cady Roberts* also rejected the contention that the obligation to disclose material information only applied where there were face-to-face dealings: "It would be anomalous indeed if the protection afforded by the antifraud provisions were withdrawn from transactions effected on exchanges, primary markets for securities transactions."

What is "Material" Information? There was no question that the dividend cut, in *Cady Roberts,* and the reduced earnings, in *Investors Management,* were "material" in the sense that they would affect the willingness of an investor to buy or sell the stock at the current price. In *Texas Gulf Sulphur,* however, the defendants argued that the information about the ore discovery did not become "material" until further drilling established the existence of a commercially mineable ore body. They pointed to the SEC's own rules under Regulation A, prohibiting a company from making any statement about the existence of an ore body unless it was sufficiently tested to be properly classified as "proven" or "probable". The court held, however, that the test of "materiality" for Rule 10b–5 purposes was not whether the company would be permitted to disclose the information if it were selling securities, but whether it was the kind of information that might affect the judgment of reasonable investors, including "speculative" as well as "conservative" investors. On this question, the court found that the size and timing of the purchases, by the defendants, some of whom had never owned TGS stock, were "highly pertinent evidence and the only truly objective evidence of the materiality of the discovery." See also SEC v. Shapiro, 494 F. 2d 1301 (2d Cir. 1974).

When is Information "Non-Public"? Under *Texas Gulf Sulphur,* an insider may not act at the moment the company makes a public announcement of the information, but must wait "until the news could reasonably have been expected to appear over the media of widest circulation." In *Investors Management,* defendants argued that the information about the company's reduced earnings was already "public" because it was the subject of rumors circulating in the financial community. The Commission held, however, that the information they received was different from the information previously circulating, since it was (a) more specific and (b) more trustworthy, having come from a firm known to be acting as underwriter for the company.

Who is an "Insider"? *Cady Roberts* established that Rule 10b–5, unlike SEA § 16(b), extends beyond officers, directors, and major stockholders to anyone who receives information from a corporate source. *Texas Gulf Sulphur* made clear that a person who passes on inside information to another person who effects a transaction is as culpable as a person who utilizes it for his own account, and *Investors Management* established the liability of the indirect "tippee", no matter how many links there are in the chain of information.

Scienter. In *Investors Management,* the Commission rejected the contention that, in order to violate Rule 10b–5, a tippee must have "actual knowledge that the information was disclosed in a breach of fiduciary duty," and held that it was sufficient that the tippee "know or have reason to know that it was non-public and had been obtained improperly by selective revelation or otherwise." The Commission indicated that liability would also attach where the tippee "knew or had reason to know that the information was obtained by industrial espionage, commercial bribery or the like." The recent Equity Funding scandal raises the (as yet unanswered) question whether someone violates the rule by selling on the basis of adverse information received from a disgruntled former employee of the company, which is vehemently denied by the company's management but subsequently turns out to be true.

In *Texas Gulf Sulphur,* the court went so far as to hold that even an insider's good faith belief that the information was already public was not a defense to an SEC enforcement action under Rule 10b–5, where there was no reasonable basis for that belief.

Causation. In *Investors Management,* the Commission held that where various factors might have affected a tippee's decision to buy or sell, it is only necessary to show that the inside information was "*a* factor" in the decision, and that "where a transaction of the kind indicated by the information is effected by the recipient prior to its public dissemination, an inference arises that the information was such a factor."

Countervailing Fiduciary Obligations. In *Texas Gulf Sulphur,* defendants argued that they could not disclose the information about the ore discovery because the corporation was engaged in acquiring options to purchase the land surrounding the exploration site. The court, while considering this a "legitimate corporate objective" (itself an interesting commentary on the differing standards in land transactions and securities transactions) held that it was "no justification" for trading; if the insiders could not disclose, they "should have kept out of the market until disclosure was accomplished."

In *Cady Roberts,* defendant argued that he had a fiduciary obligation to his customers to sell for their account when he came into possession of adverse information. The Commission rejected this defense: "clients may not expect of a broker the benefits of his inside information at the expense of the public generally." This may create a dilemma for brokers. In Slade v. Shearson, Hammill & Co., CCH ¶ 94,329 (S.D.N.Y.1974), plaintiff alleged that Shearson had solicited customer purchases of Tidal Marine stock at a time when it was in possession of material non-public adverse information which it had received from Tidal Marine in its capacity as an investment banker for that company. Shearson moved for summary judgment, arguing that under the SEC's interpretations of Rule 10b–5, "even if Shearson's corporate finance department had known this non-public information, it was precluded from using it to prevent the solicitation of purchases by its retail sales force until the information was made public." The court denied the motion, holding that prior decisions under Rule 10b–5 held only that inside information could not be disclosed to favored customers, and that its fiduciary obligations to its customers required it to refrain from making affirmative recommendations under the circumstances.

To deal with this problem, many commercial banks and broker-dealers have established "Chinese walls" barring communication between their commercial banking or underwriting departments, on the one side, and their investment advisory or sales departments, on the other, to prevent the transmission of "inside" information and the liabilities that may result from its use or non-use.

(b) Civil Liability

As noted above, a violation of Rule 10b–5 has been held to give rise to a private right of action by a person who can show that the violator invaded an interest of his which the rule was designed to protect. As applied to insider trading, this doctrine has raised difficult questions. The nature of the questions differs depending on (a) whether the transaction involved direct dealings or is effected through the impersonal facilities of an exchange, and (b) whether the right is being asserted by the person on the other side of the transaction or by or on behalf of the corporation.

Claims by the Seller (Purchaser). The operative provisions of Rule 10b–5 are worded in terms of "fraud or deceit". A common law action for deceit requires a showing of (a) false representation of fact, (b) knowledge by D that it is false (scienter), (c) intention to induce P to act, (d) justifiable reliance by P, and (e) damage to P. See W. Prosser, Torts 685–86 (4th ed. 1971). The decisions involving civil liabilities for violation of Rule 10b–5 have evidenced a progressive dilution of these requirements.

Direct Dealings. In List v. Fashion Park, 340 F.2d 457 (2d Cir. 1965), plaintiff authorized his broker to sell shares at not less than $18 a share. Defendant, acting through his own broker, purchased the shares at $18.50 and plaintiff subsequently sued him, alleging that defendant had failed to disclose (a) that he was a director of the company and (b) that negotiations were pending that eventually resulted in a merger of the company that caused the stock to be worth

$50 a share. The court held, first, that, in order to recover, plaintiff was not required to show an affirmative misrepresentation; non-disclosure of a material fact was sufficient under clause (3) of Rule 10b–5. Second, to show reliance, plaintiff need only show that the undisclosed facts would have affected his judgment (i. e., the "materiality" test, with plaintiff substituted for the "reasonable investor"). However, the court found that the facts as known to the defendant at the time of the transaction would not have affected the plaintiff's judgment, and denied him recovery. (The court was obviously impressed by the fact that the defendant had resold most of the shares at a profit of only $1 a share.)

In Affiliated Ute Citizens v. U. S., 406 U.S. 128 (1972), the Supreme Court collapsed the requirements still further. Defendants had purchased shares of the Ute Development Corporation from members of the tribe without telling them that the shares were then trading at higher prices in another market. The Court held that defendants had no right to remain silent:

"Under the circumstances of this case, involving primarily a failure to disclose, positive proof of reliance is not a prerequisite to recovery. All that is necessary is that the facts withheld be material in the sense that a reasonable investor might have considered them important in the making of this decision. This obligation to disclose and this withholding of a material fact establish the requisite element of causation in fact."

Stock Exchange Transactions. When an "insider" buys or sells on a stock exchange without disclosing material facts, there is an additional problem. Not only will there be nobody on the other side of the market who can show "reliance" in the traditional sense; there will normally be nobody who is able to trace the shares he had sold or bought to the defendant.

In 1952, the Second Circuit affirmed a decision that plaintiffs who purchased shares on an exchange in November and December could not recover damages from insiders who had sold on the exchange between March and October and had failed to disclose material adverse information. The court said that a "semblance of privity" between the seller and the buyer was required. Joseph v. Farnsworth Radio & Television Corp., 99 F.Supp. 701 (S.D.N.Y.1951), aff'd, 198 F.2d 883 (2d Cir. 1952).

In 1974, the Second Circuit reversed this position and held that privity was not required in an insider trading case under Rule 10b–5. It held that a class action could be brought on behalf of all persons who purchased stock of a company on an exchange during the period that defendants were selling that stock on the basis of inside in-

formation. Shapiro v. Merrill Lynch, 495 F.2d
228 (2d Cir. 1974). With respect to defendant's
argument that their sales could not be said to
have "caused" plaintiffs' losses, the court simply
cited *Affiliated Ute* for the proposition that the
nondisclosure of material information established
the requisite element of causation in fact.

The *Shapiro* decision of course raises a difficult
question of damages. The court recognized that
if damages were measured by the "losses" suffered by all members of the class, the liability
would be "Draconian", and left to the district
court "the fashioning of appropriate relief, including the proper measure of damages." On remand, the district court held that the class of
persons entitled to sue should include all those
who purchased between the time the defendants
started trading and the time the correct information was made public. It reasoned that limiting
the class to those who were buying at the time
the defendants were selling would re-establish the
requirement of "privity" which the court of appeals had rejected. Shapiro v. Merrill Lynch,
CCH ¶ 95,377 (S.D.N.Y.1975).

The problem of "Draconian liability" raised by
the *Shapiro* decision has led the Sixth Circuit to
a different result. In Fridrich v. Bradford, 542
F.2d 307 (6th Cir. 1976), that court held that insiders who bought in the open market on the basis of non-public information were not liable to

persons selling in the open market during the same period on the ground that "defendants' act of trading with third persons was not causally connected with any claimed loss by plaintiffs who traded on the impersonal market and who were otherwise unaffected by the wrongful acts of the insider." *Affiliated Ute* was distinguished on the basis of the face-to-face dealings and the pre-existing relationship between the parties.

Recovery by the Company. One element of the obligation under Rule 10b–5 to refrain from trading on inside information is "the existence of a relationship giving access to information intended to be available only for a corporate purpose and not for the personal benefit of anyone." Cady Roberts & Co., *supra.* It would therefore seem that the company (or a shareholder suing derivatively on its behalf) should have a right of action under Rule 10b–5 to recover the insider's trading profits, at least where the information he used was intended solely for corporate purposes. However, the one significant court-imposed limitation on private rights of action under Rule 10b–5, recently reaffirmed by the Supreme Court, is that the person bringing the action must be a "purchaser" or "seller" of securities in the transaction in question. The courts have accordingly held that the issuer may not sue to recover an insider's trading profits under Rule 10b–5. See e. g., Davidge v. White, 377 F.Supp. 1084 (S.D.N.Y. 1974).

There are, however, three alternative ways in which the insider's profits may be recovered by the corporation. First, they may be recoverable under SEA § 16(b). However, this will only apply if the insider is an officer, director or 10% shareholder, and if there was a matching purchase and sale within a six-month period.

Second, where the SEC brings an injunctive action against an insider for trading in violation of Rule 10b–5, it may request, and the court may grant, as "ancillary relief", a decree ordering the defendant to turn over his profits to the company, "subject to disposition in such manner as the court may direct." See SEC v. Texas Gulf Sulphur Co., 312 F.Supp. 77 (S.D.N.Y.1970), aff'd, 446 F.2d 1301 (2d Cir. 1971); SEC v. Golconda Mining Co., 327 F.Supp. 257 (S.D.N.Y.1971).

Third, in certain states, a corporation may be able to recover insider trading profits of its officers or directors under common law agency principles of fiduciary duty. See Diamond v. Oreamuno, 24 N.Y.2d 494, 301 N.Y.S.2d 78, 248 N.E. 2d 901 (1969); Brophy v. Cities Service Co., 31 Del.Ch. 241, 70 A.2d 5 (1949); Rest.2d, Agency § 388, Comment c. However, efforts to extend this liability to persons who trade on the basis of tips received from corporate officers have thus far been unsuccessful. See Schein v. Chasen, 313 So.2d 739 (Fla.1975); Frigitemp Corp. v. Financial Dynamics Fund, 524 F.2d 275 (2d Cir. 1975).

§ 20. Corporate Misstatements

The specific disclosure requirements of SEA §§ 13 and 14 apply only to reports, proxy statements and other documents filed with the SEC by companies which have securities registered under SEA § 12. The provisions of SEA § 10(b) and Rule 10b–5, however, are applicable to any statement, in the form of a report, press release or other document, made by any issuer.

(a) Elements of the Violation

The "In Connection With" Requirement. In SEC v. Texas Gulf Sulphur, 401 F.2d 833 (2d Cir. 1968), the Commission argued that TGS had violated Rule 10b–5(2) by issuing a press release which described the current status of its exploration of a potential ore body in an unduly pessimistic manner. TGS argued that the press release was not subject to Rule 10b–5 because it was not issued "in connection with the purchase or sale of any security", since the company was not engaged in buying or selling any securities at the time. The court held, however, that the requirement was satisfied if there was a connection between the statement and transactions by and among members of the public, i. e., if it was "of a sort that would cause reasonable investors to rely thereon, and, in connection therewith, so relying, cause them to purchase or sell a corporation's securities."

To come under Rule 10b–5, it is not even necessary that the statement be made for the purpose of influencing public investors. A company's nondisclosure of potential liability on government contracts was held to be subject to Rule 10b–5 because of its potential effect on investors, even though the statement was concededly made for the purpose of defrauding the government and not to mislead shareholders. Heit v. Weitzen, 402 F.2d 909 (2d Cir. 1968).

In *Texas Gulf Sulphur*, the court said that the first question in determining whether a corporate statement violated Rule 10b–5 was whether it was "misleading to the reasonable investor." On remand, the district court, after receiving conflicting testimony from about 30 witnesses, some of whom thought the release was pessimistic and some of whom thought it was optimistic, found that "some reasonable investors, exercising due care, were misled by the press release." SEC v. Texas Gulf Sulphur Co., 312 F.Supp. 77 (S.D.N.Y.1970), aff'd, 446 F.2d 1301 (2d Cir. 1971).

If the statement was found to be misleading, the court held that the company would have violated Rule 10b–5 if "its issuance resulted from a lack of due diligence", importing the affirmative defense found in SA § 11 (see § 11(b) *supra*). The court took care to state that this "due diligence" or "negligence" standard was applicable in an SEC action for injunctive relief, and that a higher degree of culpability would be required if the company was being sued for damages. (The Supreme Court has subsequently held in Ernst & Ernst v. Hochfelder, § 39(b) *infra*, that scienter is required in an action for damages under Rule 10b–5, and a similar requirement may also apply in SEC injunctive actions. See § 33 *infra*.)

(b) Civil Liability

The circumstances under which public investors can recover damages from a company when they purchase or sell securities on the basis of a misleading press release have not been authoritatively determined, since most of the cases have been settled. The Texas Gulf Sulphur litigation, for example, was settled by TGS paying $2,200,000 into a fund to pay claims of people who sold TGS stock after the issuance of the misleading press release and prior to the issuance of a clarifying release four days later. Cannon v. Texas Gulf Sulphur Co., CCH ¶ 93,342 (S.D.N. Y.1972).

Culpability. In a separate action against TGS brought by investors in Utah, the court held the company liable for damages. It held that "while some degree of scienter is required, it does not equate with the intent to defraud required in a common law fraud action" and that "the press release issued by defendants was misleading, intentionally deceptive, inaccurate and knowingly deficient in material facts." Mitchell v. Texas Gulf Sulphur Co., 446 F.2d 90 (10th Cir. 1971). See Ernst & Ernst v. Hochfelder, § 39(b) *infra*.

Reliance. Another unresolved question is whether an investor must prove that he relied on the company's statement in buying or selling the security. At least one court has held that he need not do so, on the theory that the damage results from his buying or selling at a price which was affected by the misstatement. Reeder v. Mastercraft Electronics Corp., 363 F.Supp. 574 (S.D.N.Y.1973).

Failure to Make a Statement. Can a company be held liable under Rule 10b–5 for failing to make a statement correcting prior statements which are no longer accurate? In Financial Industrial Fund v. McDonnell Douglas Corp., 474 F.2d 514 (10th Cir. 1973), a mutual fund sued for losses of $700,000 on its purchase of Douglas stock, alleging that the company had withheld an announcement of reduced earnings beyond the point in time at which the relevant facts were available to it. The court of appeals reversed a jury verdict for the plaintiff, holding that there was no proof that Douglas had unduly delayed its announcement. On the other hand, a company was held liable to investors under Rule 10b–5 where it failed to take action to correct misleading estimates of its earnings which were being disseminated by the principal dealer in its stock. Green v. Jonhop, 358 F.Supp. 413 (D.Ore.1973).

Overlap With Other Provisions. Since Rule 10b–5 applies to all sales as well as purchases of securities, a plaintiff may attempt to invoke it when suing on a transaction to which specific civil liability provisions of the securities laws are also applicable. Examples would be a 1933 Act registration statement subject to SA § 11, or a misleading offering circular subject to SA § 12(2). A plaintiff might invoke Rule 10b–5 to avoid the statute of limitations in SA § 13 or the provision for security for expenses in SA § 11(e). In general, the courts have held that plaintiffs have the alternative of suing under Rule 10b–5 if they assume the additional burden of alleging and proving some kind of "fraud", i. e., they cannot simply allege a violation of Rule 10b–5(2), which imposes a nonfraud standard similar to those found in SA §§ 11 and 12(2). See Stewart v. Bennett, 359 F. Supp. 878 (D.Mass.1973) and cases cited therein. One court has held that there is no implied right of action under Rule 10b–5 for a misstatement in a document filed with the SEC under the 1934 Act, as to which SEA § 18 provides an express right of action for damages. Kulchok v. Government Employees Ins. Co., CCH ¶ 96,002 (D.D.C. 1977).

§ 21. Corporate Mismanagement

One of the most important and controversial, applications of SEA Rule 10b–5 has been in the area of abuses by corporate management or controlling shareholders that may also constitute violations of their fiduciary duties under state corporation law.   Minority shareholders, suing individually, in class actions, or derivatively on behalf of the corporation, have brought actions under Rule 10b–5 to avoid substantive or procedural obstacles in state law.   Among the types of transactions which have been attacked are sales of controlling stock interests at a premium, mergers or reorganizations, and sales and purchases by corporations of their own or other securities. These complex transactions have given rise to a number of difficult questions as to the scope of the rule.

(a) Elements of the Violation

"Purchase or Sale".   One question that can arise is whether the transaction being attacked is a "purchase" or "sale".   In its first decision interpreting Rule 10b–5, the Supreme Court held that a merger involved a "sale" of the stock of the disappearing company and a "purchase" of the stock of the surviving company for the purposes of the rule.   SEC v. National Securities, 393 U.S. 453 (1969).   A recent court of appeals decision held that a spin-off by a corporation to its shareholders of its stock in a subsidiary constitutes a "sale" in light of the "umbrella of protection placed over securities transactions by § 10(b)".   International Controls Corp. v. Vesco,

490 F.2d 1334 (2d Cir. 1974). One judge, dissenting, thought the majority's interpretation "not only strains, but flatly contradicts, the words of the statute."

On the other hand, a reorganization plan, under which shares in a railroad were exchanged for shares in a holding company which became the 100% owner of the stock of the railroad, was held not to involve a sufficient change in shareholders' interests to bring the transaction within the scope of § 10(b). In re Penn Central Securities Litigation, 494 F.2d 528 (3d Cir. 1974).

"In Connection With". While the fraud must be "in connection with the purchase or sale," it need not relate to the *terms* of the transaction. In Superintendent of Insurance v. Bankers Life and Casualty Co., 404 U.S. 6 (1971), a group which obtained control of an insurance company caused it to sell certain securities which it owned, then misappropriated the proceeds for their own benefit. The Supreme Court, reversing the court of appeals, held unanimously that "since there was a 'sale' of a security and since fraud was used 'in connection with' it, there is redress under § 10(b), whatever might be available as a remedy under state law."

(b) The "Purchaser-Seller" Requirement

The most significant court-imposed limitation on private litigation under Rule 10b–5 is the requirement that the plaintiff be either a "purchaser" or "seller" of securities in the transaction being attacked. The problem frequently arises where a minority shareholder attacks the sale of a controlling block of stock, at a premium over the current market price, as a "fraud" on the minority shareholders. In Birnbaum v. Newport Steel Corp., 193 F.2d 461 (2d Cir. 1952), one of the earliest cases under Rule 10b–5, the court held that the purpose of the rule was to protect purchasers and sellers of securities from being defrauded, and that since neither the minority shareholders nor the corporation had purchased or sold any securities, they had no cause of action. (The Second Circuit subsequently held, in a landmark decision, that the transaction attacked in *Birnbaum* involved a breach of the controlling shareholder's fiduciary duty under state law. Perlman v. Feldmann, 219 F.2d 173 (2d Cir. 1955).)

The Second Circuit, where the *Birnbaum* rule originated, has been alert to find opportunities to circumvent it in sale of control situations. Where a sale of control was followed by a tender offer and a short form merger, a minority shareholder was allowed to attack the entire transaction under Rule 10b–5, since the merger made him a "forced seller" of his shares in the acquired company. Vine v. Beneficial Finance Co., 374 F.2d 627 (2d Cir. 1967). And where a sale of control was followed by a transaction in which the corporation was allegedly caused to redeem certain securities for the purpose of removing a threat to the purchaser's control, a shareholder suing under Rule 10b–5 with respect to the second transaction was permitted to add a claim with respect to the sale of control, under the doctrine of pendent jurisdiction. Drachman v. Harvey, 453 F.2d 722 (2d Cir. 1972).

However, the basic "purchaser-seller" requirement of *Birnbaum* was recently reaffirmed by the Supreme Court in Blue Chip Stamps v. Manor Drug Stores, 421 U.S. 723 (1975). In *Blue Chip*, defendants were obliged under an antitrust decree to offer plaintiffs certain shares in a new company. Plaintiffs alleged that defendants had violated Rule 10b–5 by giving a deceptively pessimistic portrayal of the new company in the prospectus, for the purpose of inducing the plaintiff *not* to buy the shares. While the facts were highly unusual, the court rested its decision denying standing to any person other than a purchaser or seller on the broad policy ground that it would deter "vexatious litigation" which "may have a settlement value out of any proportion to its prospect of success at trial" and which may raise "many rather hazy issues of historical fact the proof of which depend[s] almost entirely on oral testimony." Justice Rehnquist's majority opinion is replete with expressions of hostility to private actions against corporate management, leading dissenting Justice Blackmun to remark that "the Court exhibits a preternatural solicitousness for corporate well-being and a seeming callousness toward the investing public quite out of keeping * * * with our own tradition and the intent of the securities laws."

(c) The "New Fraud"

A recurrent type of claim under Rule 10b–5 is a derivative suit by a minority shareholder alleging that the corporation was caused to issue its own securities for an inadequate consideration, usually for the benefit of a controlling person. As far back as 1960, it was held that a corporation which was fraudulently induced to issue its own stock for inadequate consideration was a defrauded "seller" within the protection of the rule. Hooper v. Mountain States Securities Corp., 282 F.2d 195 (5th Cir. 1960). However, this left the question of how one defrauds a corporation. If the board of directors makes the decision to issue the securities, and if some or all of the directors are participants in the alleged fraudulent scheme, who can be said to be defrauding whom?

In a pair of 1964 decisions, the Second Circuit drew the distinction that if material information is withheld from any of the directors, there can be said to be a fraud on the corporation under Rule 10b–5, but that if all the directors were in

[144]

on the scheme, there could be no deception, and the only available remedy was under state law. Compare Ruckle v. Roto American Corp., 339 F. 2d 24 (2d Cir. 1964) with O'Neill v. Maytag, 339 F.2d 764 (2d Cir. 1964).

This distinction did not make much sense, and in 1968 it was rejected in favor of a rule that fraud could be shown even where all the directors were involved. "In order to establish fraud it is surely not necessary to show that the directors deceived themselves. It must be enough to show that they deceived the shareholders, the real owners of the property with which the directors were dealing." Schoenbaum v. Firstbrook, 405 F.2d 200, 215 (2d Cir. 1968); see also Pappas v. Moss, 393 F.2d 865 (3d Cir. 1968).

Under special circumstances, fraud may even be found where all the shareholders, as well as the directors, were participants in the alleged fraudulent scheme. In Bailes v. Colonial Press, 444 F.2d 1241 (5th Cir. 1971), the court held that the issuance of shares in a closely-held corporation for fictitious consideration was a fraud under Rule 10b–5 where it was the first step in a scheme which involved a subsequent stock offering to the public.

While *Schoenbaum* and *Pappas* established that fraud on the "independent" shareholders constituted fraud on the corporation, they did not establish whether fraud could be alleged simply by asserting that the terms of the transaction were substantively unfair, or whether it was necessary to allege that there was a misstatement or withholding of material information.   In Popkin v. Bishop, 464 F.2d 714 (2d Cir. 1972), a shareholder sought to enjoin a proposed merger under Rule 10b–5 on the ground that the merger terms were "grossly inadequate," even though he "admitted that the defendants fully and fairly disclosed all material facts surrounding the merger to all interested parties."   The court held that his only remedy was under state law, and dismissed the complaint, on the ground that "in [merger] transactions, if * * * shareholder approval is fairly sought and freely given, * * * questions of the wisdom of such transactions or even their fairness become tangential at best to federal regulation."

The Supreme Court subsequently put the issue to rest in Santa Fe Industries v. Green, 97 S. Ct. 1292 (1977).   In that case, defendant, owning more than 90% of the stock of Kirby Lumber Co., merged Kirby into itself by a "short-form merger" under Delaware law, requiring action only by defendant's board of directors.   Plaintiffs, minority shareholders in Kirby, alleged that the merger was a "fraud" on them within the meaning of Rule 10b–5 since (a) there was no justifiable business purpose for the merger, and (b) they were paid only $150 a share in the merger, whereas their pro rata share of Kirby's assets amounted to $772 per share. The Supreme Court held that the essence of any action under SEA § 10(b) was "deception" or "manipulation", and that the type of management overreaching alleged in this case was not the kind of "fraud" covered by that section or any rule adopted under it. It is not yet clear to what extent this decision undercuts the rationale of the *Schoenbaum* and *Pappas* decisions, *supra*. See Goldberg v. Meridor, CCH ¶ 96,162 (2d Cir. 1977).

(d) Mergers and Tender Offers

As noted above, a merger is considered a "sale" and "purchase" within the meaning of Rule 10b–5, so that the rule is available to attack misstatements in the proxy material or other improprieties in the transaction. This may be particularly useful where the merging companies are not subject to the disclosure requirements of SEA § 14 either because they are specifically exempted from the registration requirements of SEA § 12, see SEC v. National Securities, 393 U.S. 453 (1969) (insurance companies) or because they have too few shareholders to be subject to its provisions, see Swanson v. American Consumer Industries, 475 F.2d 516 (7th Cir. 1973).

Application of the rule to merger situations involves the problem, encountered with respect to § 14, of determining whether the alleged misstatement or other violation can be said to have caused the transaction and caused the loss, although the analysis is somewhat different under the two sections. See Schlick v. Penn-Dixie Cement Corp., 507 F.2d 374 (2d Cir. 1974).

Prior to the enactment of the Williams Act in 1968, contestants in several takeover bid situations attempted to invoke Rule 10b–5 to reach alleged abuses by their adversaries. The problem was that neither the aggressor nor the target company would normally be a "purchaser" or "seller" within the meaning of *Birnbaum, supra,* see Iroquois Industries v. Syracuse China Corp., 417 F.2d 963 (2d Cir. 1969), unless it could bring itself within the "forced seller" exception, see Crane Co. v. Westinghouse Air Brake Co., 419 F. 2d 787 (2d Cir. 1969), result reversed at CCH ¶ 96,160 (S.D.N.Y.1977). While one court of appeals indicated after the passage of the Williams Act that Rule 10b–5 might still be invoked in a tender offer situation where SEA § 14(e) was unavailable, H. K. Porter Co. v. Nicholson File Co., 482 F.2d 421 (1st Cir. 1973), it seems unlikely, after the Supreme Court holdings in *Blue Chip, supra,* and *Piper,* § 15 *supra,* that any private right of action would be implied under the rule for either the aggressor or the target corporation.

V. REGULATION OF THE SECURI-TIES BUSINESS

A substantial portion of the SEC's activity is devoted to regulation of firms engaged in the securities business. The three principal capacities in which firms act in that business are as broker, dealer, and investment adviser. The 1934 Act defines a "broker" as a "person engaged in the business of effecting transactions in securities for the account of others", SEA § 3(a)(4), while a "dealer" is a "person engaged in the business of buying and selling securities for his own account", SEA § 3(a)(5). An "investment adviser" is defined in § 202(a)(11) of the Investment Advisers Act of 1940 as a "person who, for compensation, engages in the business of advising others * * * as to the advisability of investing in, purchasing or selling securities * * *."

Under SEA § 15(a), no person may engage in business as a broker or dealer (unless he does exclusively intrastate business or deals only in exempted securities) unless he is registered with the Commission. Under § 15(b), the Commission may revoke or suspend a broker-dealer's registration, or impose a censure, if the broker-dealer is found to have violated any of the federal securities laws or committed other specified misdeeds. SEA § 15B, added in 1975, and IAA § 203 contain comparable provisions with respect to municipal securities dealers and investment advisers, respectively.

§ 22.   Broker-Dealer Selling Practices

In spelling out the substantive obligations of these securities "professionals" in dealing with public investors, the Commission has proceeded largely under the general antifraud provisions of SEA §§ 10(b) and 15(c), SA § 17(a) and IAA § 206. Its attention has been focused on two broad areas: (a) conflicts between the professional's obligations to his customers and his own financial interests, and (b) trading in or recommending securities in the absence of adequate information about the issuer. Violation of the anti-fraud provisions in these two areas has given rise to lawsuits by aggrieved customers as well as disciplinary actions by the SEC.

In construing the terms "fraud" and "deceit", as applied to securities professionals, the Supreme Court has held that Congress did not use them "in their technical sense", which would require a showing of intent to injure and actual injury to clients. At least in SEC enforcement proceedings, the Court held, they should be interpreted liberally to reach all practices which create a conflict of interest between the professional and his clients. SEC v. Capital Gains Research Bureau, 375 U.S. 180 (1963).

(a) Conflicts of Interest

Conflicts of interest in the securities business arise from the fact that what is best for the broker-dealer or investment adviser is not always best for the customer. They are complicated by the fact, noted above, that securities firms often engage in several different types of activities, with differing responsibilities. In particular, many broker-dealer firms act as brokers, or agents, for their customers in purchasing or selling securities listed on a stock exchange, but also act as dealer, or principal, selling to, or buying from, their customers, securities traded in the over-the-counter (OTC) market. This tends to confuse customers, since the legal obligations of an agent to act in the best interests of his principal do not apply to a dealer who is theoretically dealing with the customers at arm's length.

In Charles Hughes & Co. v. SEC, 139 F.2d 434 (2d Cir. 1943), the court accepted the position urged by the SEC, that a broker-dealer firm which solicited business on the basis of "the confidence in itself which it managed to instill in its customers," was under a duty not to overreach its customers even when dealing with them as "principal". This has come to be known as the "shingle theory", under which a broker-dealer who hangs out his "shingle" as an expert in securities and offers advice to customers on their transactions will be held to violate the antifraud provisions of the 1933 and 1934 Acts when he deals with customers without making full disclosure of his possible conflicts of interest or other facts material to the customer's investment decision.

Excessive Prices.   The particular violation alleged by the SEC in the *Hughes* case was the sale of OTC securities to unsophisticated customers at markups ranging from 16% to 40% above their current market value, without any disclosure of that fact.   The problem of excessive charges was subsequently dealt with by the National Association of Securities Dealers (NASD), the self-regulatory organization for the OTC market.

In 1943, the NASD adopted an "interpretation" to the effect that a markup of not more than 5% would ordinarily be considered a "fair spread or profit" within the meaning of its Rules of Fair Practice.   A large number of disciplinary proceedings based wholly or partly on excessive markups have been brought against broker-dealers by both the NASD and the SEC.   Although the decisions generally refer to the "5% policy", markups between 5% and 10% may be justified in some circumstances.   Markups above 10% are generally considered unjustifiable.

Disclosure of Status.   SEA Rule 10b–10 requires a broker-dealer to furnish its customers with a written confirmation of each transaction, indicating, among other things, whether it is acting as broker for the customer, as dealer for its own account, or as broker for another person. The courts have held, however, that when a broker-dealer is acting as a "market-maker" i. e., regularly buying and selling the particular security), it must go beyond the technical disclosure required in the confirmation and make sure that the customer is fully and clearly apprised of its market-maker status. Chasins v. Smith, Barney & Co., 438 F.2d 1167 (2d Cir. 1970); Cant v. A. G. Becker & Co., 374 F.Supp. 36 (N.D.Ill.1974).

"Churning". Where a broker-dealer is the sole, or dominant, market-maker in a particular security, and creates a market in that security by repeated purchases from, and resales to, its individual retail customers at steadily increasing prices, its course of conduct will be held to violate the antifraud provisions if it does not make full disclosure to the customers of the nature of the market. Norris & Hirshberg v. SEC, 177 F.2d 228 (D.C.Cir. 1949). But a firm can also be held in violation of the antifraud provisions for "churning" a customer's account (i. e., causing the customer to engage in an excessive number of transactions) where it is acting solely as broker for the customer on a commission basis.

SEA Rule 15c1–7 makes it illegal for any broker or dealer to effect transactions in OTC securities, for any customer's account over which such broker or dealer has investment discretion, "which are excessive in size or frequency in view of the financial resources and character of the account."

"In determining whether churning has taken place, courts have looked to (1) the number and frequency of the trades, (2) the amount of 'in-and-out' trading (3) the amount of commissions generated by the trading both in dollar terms and as a percentage of the broker's salary, (4) the investor's objectives in the market and his level of business sophistication, and (5) the degree of control exercised by the securities dealer over the investment account." Horne v. Francis I. duPont & Co., 428 F.Supp. 1271 (D.D.C.1977).

"Scalping".   Another practice which the SEC has attacked as a fraud is "scalping"—a situation in which an investment adviser publicly recommends the purchase of securities without disclosing its practice of purchasing such securities before making the recommendation and then selling them at a profit when the price rises after the recommendation is disseminated.   In SEC v. Capital Gains Research Bureau, 375 U.S. 180 (1963), the Supreme Court agreed with the SEC and held such conduct to violate the antifraud provisions of the Investment Advisers Act of 1940, even though there was no allegation that the investment adviser's actions had injured its clients or that it did not believe in the recommendations it was making.   More recently, the SEC secured a con-

sent injunction under Rule 10b–5 against a newspaper columnist who engaged in similar activities, but a court subsequently held that the columnist was not, on that account, civilly liable to persons who alleged that the price at which they acquired certain shares was significantly affected by his recommendations. Zweig v. Hearst Corp., 407 F.Supp. 763 (C.D.Cal.1976).

(b) Inadequate Basis for Recommendations

An important objective of the disclosure provisions of the federal securities laws, discussed in earlier chapters, is to assure that investors, and the broker-dealers who advise them, have adequate information about the issuer to make rational investment decisions. In furtherance, or rather extension, of this approach, the SEC has taken the position that it is a violation of the antifraud provisions for a broker-dealer to recommend the purchase of a security unless it has enough reliable information about the issuer to form a sound basis for its recommendations.

The Commission initially applied this approach to "boiler-room" operations—firms set up for the sole purpose of aggressively peddling the stock of one or a few highly speculative issuers, by means of long distance telephone calls and high-pressure sales techniques. See Berko v. SEC, 316 F. 2d 137 (2d Cir. 1963), in which a "boiler-room" operator was held to have violated the Act by

making unwarranted predictions that the price of
a particular stock would rise to $15 a share with-
in a year, even though the stock did subsequently
rise to that level.

This approach was subsequently extended beyond the "boiler-room" situation to apply to all
broker-dealers. In Hanly v. SEC, 415 F.2d 589
(2d Cir. 1969), the court held that a broker-dealer which made unsubstantiated recommendations
was subject to SEC sanctions since, under the
"shingle" theory, "by his position he implicitly
represents he has an adequate basis for the opinions he renders."   The courts, however, have
been reluctant to award damages to customers
who purchase securities on the basis of such unsubstantiated recommendations, requiring some
showing of reasonable reliance on the recommendation by the customer. See Phillips v. Reynolds
& Co., 294 F.Supp. 1249 (E.D.Pa.1969).

Supplementing its proceedings against individual broker-dealers, the SEC in 1971 adopted SEA
Rule 15c2–11, which prohibits a broker-dealer
from making a market in any security unless the
issuer (a) has recently made a public offering under the 1933 Act or Regulation A or (b) is currently filing reports under the 1934 Act, or unless
(c) the broker-dealer has in its files specified
current financial and other information about the
issuer and its securities. The purpose, and effect,
of this rule is to prevent the creation of public

trading markets in securities which have not been registered under either the 1933 Act (including Regulation A) or the 1934 Act.

§ 23. Financial Responsibility of Broker-Dealers

Since many broker-dealers maintain custody of funds and securities belonging to their customers, safeguards are required to assure that the customers can recover those funds and securities in the event the broker-dealer becomes insolvent. The three principal techniques that have been utilized are (a) financial responsibility standards for broker-dealers, (b) requirements for segregation of customers' funds and securities, and (c) maintenance of an industry-wide fund to satisfy the claims of customers whose brokerage firms become insolvent.

(a) Net Capital Rules

The basic financial responsibility standards for broker-dealers are found in the "net capital" rules adopted by the SEC under authority of SEA § 15(c)(3). Prior to the financial debacle suffered by the securities industry in 1968–70, securities firms belonging to exchanges which had "net capital" rules deemed to be more stringent than those of the SEC were exempt from the SEC's requirements. However, after SEC and Congressional investigations showed how flexibly the exchanges had interpreted their rules to allow member firms to continue in business with inade-

quate capital, the SEC revoked this exemption
and made all broker-dealers subject to its requirements.

Under the SEC net capital rule, SEA Rule
15c3–1, which was substantially revised in 1975,
see SEA Rel. 11497, a broker-dealer must maintain "net capital" of at least $25,000 ($5,000 in
the case of broker-dealers which do not hold any
customers' funds or securities and conduct their
business in a specified manner). "Net capital" is
defined as "net worth" (excess of assets over liabilities), subject to many special adjustments prescribed in the rule. In addition, a broker-dealer
may not let its aggregate indebtedness exceed
1500% of its net capital (800% during its first
year of business).

A broker-dealer can alternatively qualify under
Rule 15c3–1(f), which is designed to test its general financial integrity and liquidity and its ability to meet its continuing commitments to its customers. Under this alternative, a broker-dealer
must maintain net capital equal to the greater of
$100,000 or 4% of the aggregate debit balances
attributable to its transactions with customers.

(b) Customers' Funds and Securities

Customers leave large amounts of cash and securities with their brokers. The securities are of
two types: securities purchased "on margin" (i.
e., with the broker advancing part of the pur-

chase price to the customer), which (under the standard margin agreement) the broker is entitled to hold as security for the loan and to repledge to secure its own borrowings; and "fully-paid" securities, which the broker holds solely as a convenience for the customer and is supposed to "segregate" from the broker's own securities. The cash "free credit balances" arise principally from two sources: a deposit of cash by a customer prior to giving his broker a purchase order, and receipt by the broker of proceeds of a sale of securities, or interest or dividend income, which has not yet been reinvested or delivered to the customer.

With respect to fully-paid securities, investigators of the securities industry's operational crises in 1968–70 discovered that many firms had lost control of their records, and did not have in their possession many of the securities which they were supposed to be holding as custodians for their customers. Accordingly, the SEC in 1972 adopted SEA Rule 15c3–3, which requires that all brokers "promptly obtain and * * * thereafter maintain the physical possession or control of all fully-paid securities", and prescribes daily determinations of compliance with the rule.

With respect to cash free credit balances, brokers have traditionally mingled the cash belonging to customers with their own assets used in their business. Since 1964, SEA Rule 15c3–2 has required brokers to notify their customers at least quarterly that such funds (a) are not segregated and may be used in the business, and (b) are payable to the customer on demand. In the wake of the 1968–70 debacle, which revealed that many firms had been using customers' free credit balances as their own working capital, there were demands for complete segregation of these cash balances. The industry argued, however, that it should continue to have interest-free use of these moneys (which in the years 1967–70 ranged from 2 to 3.7 *billion* dollars) to finance customer-related transactions (principally margin loans). The result was SEA Rule 15c3–3, adopted by the SEC in 1972, which requires each broker to maintain a "Special Reserve Bank Account for the Exclusive Benefit of Customers" in which it holds cash or U.S. government securities in an amount equal to (a) free credit balances in customers' accounts (plus other amounts owing to customers) less (b) debit balances in customers' cash and margin accounts.

(c) The Securities Investor Protection Act

Following the financial collapse of one of its large member firms in 1963, the NYSE established a "trust fund", financed by assessments on its members, to pay the claims of customers of member firms which failed. This trust fund proved inadequate to deal with the financial crisis of 1969–70, however, and the industry turned to

Congress to establish a more secure system of customer protection. Congress responded by passing the Securities Investor Protection Act of 1970 (SIPA).

SIPA § 3(a) created a non-profit membership corporation, called Securities Investor Protection Corporation (SIPC), and requires every broker-dealer registered under SEA § 15 (with certain limited exceptions) to be a member. The corporation is managed by a seven-person board of directors, of which one is appointed by the Secretary of the Treasury, one by the Federal Reserve Board, and five by the President, of which three are to be representatives of different segments of the securities industry and two are to be from the general public. SIPA § 3(c).

In order to accumulate the funds necessary to enable SIPC to meet its responsibilities, each member of SIPC is required to pay an annual assessment equal to $\frac{1}{2}$ of 1% of the member's gross revenues, until SIPC has accumulated a fund of $150 million, and to pay such further assessments as are necessary to maintain the fund at that level, SIPA § 4(c), (d). If this fund proves insufficient, SIPC is authorized to borrow up to $1 billion from the Treasury (through the SEC). The SEC, if it determines that assessments on members will not satisfactorily provide for repayment of the loan, may levy a charge of not more than ⅟₅₀ of 1% of all transactions in the exchange and OTC markets to provide for repayment. SIPA § 4(g).

Operation of SIPC. If the SEC or a self-regulatory organization determines that a broker or dealer is in or approaching financial difficulty, it must notify SIPC. If SIPC determines that the member has failed or is in danger of failing to meet its obligations to customers, or that certain other conditions exist, it may apply to a court for a decree adjudicating that the customers of the member are in need of the protection provided by the Act. SIPA § 5(a). A customer of a SIPC member has no right to apply to a court for an order directing SIPC to take action with respect to that member. SIPC v. Barbour, 421 U.S. 412 (1975).

If the court makes the requisite findings and issues the requested decree, it must then appoint as trustee, and attorney for the trustee, "disinterested" persons designated by SIPC. SIPA § 5(b)(3). The functions of the trustee are (a) to return "specifically identifiable property" to customers and to satisfy their other claims out of available funds, (b) to complete the "open contractual commitments" of the firm, and (c) to liquidate the firm's business. If the firm's assets are insufficient to satisfy the claims of all customers, SIPC must advance to the trustee moneys sufficient to satisfy all such claims, up to a maximum of $50,000 for each customer (but not more than $20,000 in respect of claims for cash). SIPA § 6(a), (f). In general, the liquidation proceeding is to be conducted in the same manner as if it were being conducted under Chapter X of the Bankruptcy Act. SIPA § 6(c).

A number of difficult problems have arisen in the administration of the Act, particularly with respect to prompt settlement of customers' claims, and proposals have been made for substantial revisions of the procedural requirements.

§ 24. Market Regulation

In addition to its provisions for the regulation of individual broker-dealers, the Securities Exchange Act regulates the overall operations of the markets in which securities are traded. The principal regulatory provisions included in the original act in 1934 were §§ 7 and 8, governing the extension of credit on listed securities, and § 11, regulating trading by exchange members for their own account. These provisions have been substantially modified over the years. In the Securities Acts Amendments of 1975, Congress also added §§ 11A and 17A, directing the SEC to facilitate the establishment of a "national market system" and a national system for clearing and settlement of transactions.

(a) Extension of Credit

"For the purpose of preventing the excessive use of credit for the purchase or carrying of securities," SEA §§ 7 and 8 authorize the Federal Reserve Board (FRB) to limit "the amount of credit that may be initially extended and subsequently maintained on any security," and to regulate borrowing by brokers and dealers. Pursuant to this authority, the FRB has promulgated regulations governing the extension of credit by broker-dealers (Regulation T), banks (Regulation U), and other persons (Regulation G), and the obtaining of credit by purchasers (Regulation X). See 12 C.F.R. pts. 220, 221, 207, 224.

While SEA § 7 authorizes the FRB to regulate both the initial extension and the subsequent maintenance of credit, the FRB rules, or "margin regulations," as they are generally known, in fact regulate only the initial extension of credit on a new purchase. See 12 C.F.R. § 220.7(b). This is done by specification of a "maximum loan value" of securities, expressed as a percentage of current value, which the FRB changes from time to time in response to increases and decreases in the amount of speculative activity and the availability of credit. For example, if the current "maximum loan value" is 50%, a customer who wants to buy securities with a current market value of $4,000 must put up $2,000 in cash and may borrow the remaining $2,000 from his broker "on margin." If the securities subsequently decline in value to $2,500, the FRB margin regulations would not require the customer to pay an additional $750 to the broker to reduce his debt to $1,250. However, certain stock exchanges do impose "margin maintenance" rules on their members, requiring that customers maintain a "margin," or equity, in their accounts equal to at least 25% of current market value. See, e. g., NYSE Rule 431(b). Thus, if the broker in this example was an NYSE member, it would be required to make a "margin call" on the customer to reduce his loan by $125, thus raising his "margin" to $625, or 25% of current market value. If the customer then wanted to buy another $2,500 worth of securities, the FRB margin regulations would require him to put up $1,875 in cash, since he could only borrow an additional $625 from the broker—the difference between the maximum loan value of the account ($2,500) and his outstanding loan to the broker ($1,875).

The FRB restrictions apply only to extension of credit on equity securities; there are no limitations on the amount of credit that may be extended for the purchase of U.S. government bonds, state and local government bonds, or nonconvertible corporate debt securities. SEA § 7(a); 12 C.F.R. § 220.4(i). As originally enacted, SEA § 7 permitted extension of credit only on equity securities listed on a stock exchange; over-the-counter stocks had no "loan value." However, the statute was amended in 1968 to permit extension of credit on OTC stocks meeting criteria established by the FRB, which maintains a list of such securities. See 12 C.F.R. § 220.-2(e). SEA § 11(d) bars broker-dealers from extending any credit to customers for the purchase of newly-issued securities with respect to which the broker-dealer is acting as an underwriter or selling group member.

While the power to regulate extensions of credit under SEA §§ 7 and 8 is vested in the FRB, enforcement of the rules with respect to broker-dealers is the responsibility of the SEC and the self-regulatory organizations. A large number of proceedings have been brought against broker-dealers for violations of the margin rules, which bar them not only from extending credit in violation of FRB limitations but also from arranging for the extension of such credit by others. SEA § 7(c); 12 C.F.R. § 220.7(a).

Although the basic purpose of the margin regulations is to restrict stock market speculation, rather than to protect individual customers, some courts have allowed customers to sue their brokers for losses on transactions in which the brokers extended credit in violation of the rules, even where the illegal extension of credit was not shown to have induced the customer to enter into the transaction. Pearlstein v. Scudder & German, 429 F.2d 1136 (2d Cir. 1970), modified at 527 F.2d 1141 (2d Cir. 1975). However, the addition in 1970 of SEA § 7(f), prohibiting *customers* from obtaining credit in violation of the FRB rules, coupled with the Supreme Court's current reluctance to imply new private rights of action, has led the courts in the more recent cases to deny customers any right to recover in these circumstances. See Utah State University v. Bear Stearns & Co., 549 F.2d 164 (10th Cir. 1977); Drasner v. Thomson McKinnon Securities, Inc., 433 F.Supp. 485 (S.D.N.Y.1977).

Disclosure. Loans by securities firms to their customers are specifically exempted from the federal Truth in Lending Act. 15 U.S.C. § 1603(2). However, the exemption was premised on a Congressional understanding that the SEC would promulgate substantially similar disclosure rules under its existing authority. SEA Rule 10b–16, adopted by the SEC in 1969, requires broker-dealers to disclose to their margin customers (a) the rate and method of computing interest on their indebtedness, and (b) the nature of the firm's interest in the customer's securities and the circumstances under which additional collateral may be required. A firm which fails to disclose its policy with respect to requirement of additional collateral may be liable to a customer for damages resulting from the customer's failure to meet a margin call. Liang v. Dean Witter, 540 F.2d 1107 (D.C.Cir. 1976).

(b) Trading by Exchange Members

The principal function, and purpose, of a national securities exchange is to provide a marketplace in which member firms, acting as brokers, can purchase and sell securities for the account of their customers. The question addressed in SEA § 11 is the extent to which stock exchange members and their firms should be permitted to trade in listed securities for their own account, in view of the possibly unfair advantages they may have over public customers when engaging in such trading.

SEA § 11(a), as amended in 1975, prohibits an exchange member from effecting any transactions on the exchange for its own account, or any account with respect to which it exercises investment discretion, with certain specified exceptions, including transactions as a market maker (specialist) or odd-lot dealer, stabilizing transactions in connection with distributions (see § 17(a) *supra*), bona fide arbitrage transactions, and other transactions which the SEC concludes should be exempt from the prohibition.

Traditionally, the inquiry has focused on three special categories of transactions: (a) "floor trading" and "off-floor trading" by members and their firms, (b) transactions by "odd-lot dealers," and (c) transactions by specialists. More recently, the increasing domination of NYSE trading by institutional customers has focused attention on two additional categories: (d) "block positioning" by member firms, and (e) transactions for "managed institutional accounts."

"Floor Trading" and "Off-Floor Trading."   The principal purpose of SEA § 11(a), as originally enacted, was to authorize the SEC to write rules (1) "to regulate or prevent floor trading" by exchange members, and (2) to prevent excessive off-floor trading by members if the Commission found it "detrimental to the maintenance of a fair and orderly market."

"Floor trading" was the speciality of a small percentage of NYSE members who maintained their memberships for the sole or primary purpose of roaming around the exchange floor and trading for their own account in whatever securities caught their fancy.   The SEC adopted some mild restrictions on floor trading in 1945, but nothing significant was done until 1963, when the Commission's Special Study of the Securities Markets concluded that floor trading was a vestige of the pre-1934 "private club" atmosphere of the exchanges, and should be abolished.   In 1964, the Commission adopted a rule prohibiting all floor trading by members, unless conducted in accordance with a plan adopted by an exchange and approved by the Commission.   SEA Rule 11a–1. The NYSE simultaneously adopted a plan, which was then approved by the Commission, requiring floor traders to register with the exchange, to maintain minimum capital and pass a qualifying examination, and to comply with special restrictions on their trading activity.   See NYSE Rules

110–112. Floor trading currently accounts for less than ½ of 1% of NYSE trading.

"Off-floor" trading by member firms (i. e. transactions initiated by decisions at the firm's offices, rather than on the floor), accounts for about ten times as much activity as floor trading, having amounted to roughly 4–5% of total NYSE volume for many years. This type of activity has not been thought to give rise to the same kind of problems as floor trading, and the SEC has never undertaken to impose any direct restrictions on it. However, after an SEC study of off-floor trading in 1967, the NYSE adopted rules designed to prevent member firms from transmitting orders to the floor ahead of their customers at times when they might be privy to "inside information." CCH NYSE Guide ¶ 2112.10.

"Odd Lots." The normal unit of trading in shares on an exchange is 100 shares (a "round lot"). Transactions involving less than 100 shares ("odd lots") are not handled through the normal trading process. Traditionally, a broker wishing to sell (or buy) an odd lot for a customer on the NYSE would sell it to one of two firms which specialized in odd lots, for a price equal to the price of the next trade in a round lot of the same security, less a "differential" of 12½¢ or 25¢ a share, depending on the price of the stock. As the odd lot firm built up a positive or negative balance in a stock through these transactions, it

would offset it through round lot transactions on the exchange for its own account.

After an abortive antitrust suit against the two firms, alleging that they had conspired to fix the odd-lot differential, see Eisen v. Carlisle & Jacquelin, 417 U.S. 156 (1974), the two firms merged. More recently, some of the largest brokerage firms have begun handling their customers' odd lots by buying or selling them as principal for their own account, without routing them to the NYSE floor.

Specialists. The specialist firm occupies a unique dual role in the operation of the NYSE and other exchanges. First, it acts as a "broker's broker," maintaining a "book" on which other brokers can leave customers' "limit orders" (i. e., orders to buy or sell at a price at which they cannot currently be executed). Second, it acts as the exclusive franchised dealer, or "market maker" in its assigned stocks, buying and selling shares from other brokers when there are no customer orders on its book against which they can be matched.

The functions of the specialist can be illustrated by the following example. A firm is the specialist in an actively-traded stock, in which the market is 40–40⅛. This means that customer orders are on the specialist's book to buy specified numbers of shares at $40 or less, and other orders are on his book to sell at $40⅛ or more (for historical reasons, shares are quoted in halves, quarters and eighths, rather than cents, and the minimum unit is ⅛ point, or 12½ cents). A broker who comes to the specialist with an order to sell "at the market" will sell to the customer with the first buy order on the book at $40, and a broker who comes with a market order to buy will buy from the customer with the first sell order on the book at 40⅛. The specialist acts solely as a subagent, receiving a portion of the "book" customer's commission to his broker.

Now assume the same firm is also specialist in an inactively traded stock. The only orders on the book are an order to buy at 38 and an order to sell at 42. If the specialist acted solely as agent, a broker who came in with a market order to sell would receive 38, and another broker who came in an hour later with a market order to buy would pay 42. The report of these two trades on the "tape" would indicate the stock had risen 4 points, or 10%, in an hour. The exchange therefore imposes an obligation on the specialist to maintain an "orderly market" in his assigned stocks, buying and selling for his own account to even out swings which would result from buyers and sellers not appearing at his post at the same time. In this case he might make his market at 40–40¼, trading for his own account as long as necessary, but yielding priority to customers' orders on his book whenever they provide as good a price to the party on the other side.

While this combination of functions has obvious advantages, it also offers possibilities for abuse. With his monopoly trading position and knowledge of the "book," the specialist, by moving the price of his specialty stocks up and down, can guarantee himself profits in both his "broker" and "dealer" functions. The SEC has from time to time studied, and expressed its concern about, this problem, but has never undertaken direct regulation of specialists' activities. In 1965, it adopted SEA Rule 11b–1, requiring the principal exchanges to maintain and enforce rules designed to curb abuses by specialists, but recent SEC and Congressional studies have expressed continuing dissatisfaction with NYSE surveillance and regulation of specialist activities. Starting in 1976, however, the NYSE has disciplined a number of specialists for improper trades or reports of trades, failure to maintain orderly markets, and other violations.

In 1975, Congress amended SEA § 11(b) to make clear that the SEC had authority to limit specialists to acting either as brokers or dealers, but not both, but the Commission has not yet taken any action pursuant to this authority.

"Block Positioning." Institutional investors (principally pension funds, mutual funds, and insurance companies) have increased their investments in common stocks to the point that they currently account for 60–70% of the trading on

the New York Stock Exchange. Institutions often trade in large blocks (10,000 shares or more) which put special strains on exchange market-making mechanisms. If a member firm which specializes in institutional business has a customer which wishes to sell 100,000 shares of a particular stock, but can only find buyers for 80,000, the firm itself will "position" the remaining 20,000 shares, and then sell them off over a period of time as the market can absorb them. SEA § 11(a)(1)(A) recognizes this "market making" function as a legitimate exception to the prohibition against trading by members for their own account; however, NYSE Rule 438 bars member firms from going into full competition with the specialist by publishing simultaneous bid and asked prices for the same stock.

"Institutional Membership." Another question raised by the growth of institutional trading was whether an institution (or an affiliated broker) should be permitted to become a member of an exchange to effect transactions for the institution's account. The NYSE has consistently barred institutions and their affiliates from membership. However, a number of institutions, in the pre-1975 period when fixed minimum commissions were charged on all stock exchange transactions, joined "regional" exchanges (which serve as alternative markets for most NYSE-listed stocks) to achieve greater flexibility in the use

of their commission dollars, or to recover a portion of the commissions for the benefit of the institutions.

The brokerage firms, alarmed at the potential loss of their biggest customers, persuaded Congress in the 1975 amendments to prevent "institutional membership" by prohibiting any exchange member from effecting any transaction on the exchange for any institutional account over which it or an affiliate exercises investment discretion. However, since the elimination of fixed rates in 1975 eliminated virtually all incentive for institutions to join exchanges, the brokerage firms discovered that they (or those of them that manage institutional accounts) were the principal victims of the new prohibition, and have been attempting to persuade Congress and the SEC to lift the ban. See SEA Rel. 13388 (1977).

(c) Market Structure

The fixed minimum commission rates maintained by the New York Stock Exchange prior to 1975 resulted in the diversion of a substantial portion of institutional trading to the "regional" exchanges or to the "third market" (an over-the-counter market in NYSE-listed stocks, maintained by non-member market makers). This "fragmentation" results in orders for a single stock being routed to different markets, with customers in some cases receiving less favorable prices than they would have received if all orders met in a single place.

Accordingly, in the Securities Acts Amendments of 1975, Congress directed the SEC to "use its authority to facilitate the establishment of a national market system" to link all markets for particular securities. SEA § 11A. The principal tangible result of this effort to date has been the consolidation of the stock exchange "tape" so that it records all transactions in a listed security, wherever effected. Efforts to consolidate the market making function in a single facility have thus far foundered on the fact that NYSE specialists, regional exchange specialists, and "third market" dealers all operate in different ways, and no satisfactory formula has yet been devised to assure "equal regulation" of their varied activities within a single system.

(d) Clearing and Settlement

Congressional and SEC investigations of the securities industry's "paperwork crisis" during the period from 1968 to 1970 revealed that a substantial cause of the problem was the obsolete and inefficient method of completing transactions by the delivery (and, in some cases, cancellation and reissuance) of stock certificates. Accordingly, in the Securities Act Amendments of 1975, Congress directed the SEC to "use its authority to facilitate the establishment of a national system for the prompt and accurate clearance and settlement of transactions in securities." SEA § 17A(a). In furtherance of this objective, the SEC was given direct regulatory power over clearing agencies and transfer agents, SEA § 17A(b), (c), as well as the power to prescribe the format of securities registered under the 1934 Act. SEA § 12(*l*).

Since the crisis, transfers of certificates have been reduced somewhat by the establishment of a depository through which certain major brokers and banks can effect transfers among themselves without movement of certificates. Also the SEC in 1977 prescribed a set of minimum performance standards for transfer agents. See SEA Rules 17Ad–1 *et seq.* However, efforts to develop a single rational and efficient system for clearing all securities transactions have been hampered by rivalry between banks and brokers, between banks in New York and those in other cities, and between clearing systems maintained by various stock exchanges and other entities.

§ 25. "Self-Regulation"

The scheme of regulation of the securities business is complicated by the fact that regulatory authority is not lodged solely in the SEC, but is divided between the SEC and a number of "self-regulatory organizations" (SRO). These are private associations of broker-dealers to which Congress has delegated (a) authority to adopt and enforce rules for the conduct of their members and (b) responsibility to assure compliance by their members with provisions of the federal securities laws.

Stock Exchanges.   When Congress created the SEC in 1934, stock exchanges, as private associations, had been regulating their members for up to 140 years.   Rather than displace this system of "self-regulation", Congress superimposed the SEC on it as an additional level of regulation. SEA § 5 requires every "national securities exchange" to register with the SEC.   Under SEA § 6(b), an exchange cannot be registered unless the SEC determines that its rules are designed, among other things, to "prevent fraudulent and manipulative acts and practices, to promote just and equitable principles of trade," and to provide for appropriate discipline of its members for any violations of its own rules or the securities laws.

Under this authority, the various exchanges, of which the New York Stock Exchange (NYSE) is by far the largest and most important, have maintained and enforced a large body of rules for the conduct of their members.   These rules fall into two categories: rules relating to transactions on the particular exchange, and rules relating to the internal operations of the member firms and their dealings with their customers.

In the first group are found rules governing: criteria for listing securities on the exchange and provisions for delisting or suspension of trading in particular securities; obligations of issuers of listed securities; bids and offers on the exchange floor; activities of "specialists" (designated market-makers in listed securities); transactions by members in listed securities for their own account; conditions under which transactions in listed securities may be effected off the exchange; clearing and settlement of exchange transactions; and rules for the governance and operation of the exchange itself.

In the second category are generally found rules governing: the form of organization of member firms and qualifications of their partners or officers; qualifications of salesmen and other personnel; handling of customers accounts; advertising; and financial statements and reports. In the case of firms which are members of more than one exchange, there is a kind of "pecking order" with respect to regulatory responsibility: the NYSE has principal responsibility for regulation of the internal affairs of all of its members (which includes almost all of the largest firms in the industry), the American Stock Exchange has principal responsibility for those of its members that are not also NYSE members, and the various "regional" exchanges in cities other than New York have responsibility over their "sole" members.

SEA § 19, as originally enacted, gave the SEC power to suspend or withdraw the registration of an exchange, to suspend or expel any member of an exchange, to suspend trading in listed securities, and to require changes in exchange rules with respect to a wide range of matters. However, it did not require SEC approval for changes in stock exchange rules, nor did it provide for SEC review of disciplinary actions by exchanges against their members.

National Association of Securities Dealers. When Congress decided to extend federal regulation over the nonexchange, or over-the-counter (OTC) market, it followed the pattern already established with respect to exchanges. SEA § 15A, added by the "Maloney Act" of 1938, authorized the establishment of "national securities associations" to be registered with the SEC. Like an exchange, any such association must have rules designed "to prevent fraudulent and manipulative acts and practices [and] to promote just and equitable principles of trade" in transactions in the OTC market. SEA § 15A(b)(6). Only one such association has been established, the National Association of Securities Dealers (NASD). The NASD has adopted a substantial body of "Rules of Fair Practice," dealing with various problems in the OTC markets. Among the most important are: its rule that a dealer may not recommend a security unless he has reason to believe it is "suitable" to the customer's financial situation and needs; its interpretation of its "fair spread or profit" rule to bar markups in excess of 5% on principal transactions (see § 22(a) *supra*); its procedures for reviewing underwriting compensation and provisions for assuring that members make a bona fide public offering of underwritten securities; and its rules with respect to execution of orders in the OTC market and disclosure in confirmations to customers.

Prior to 1971, the NASD was a purely regulatory organization, since the OTC market had no central facility comparable to an exchange floor. Trading was effected by telephone calls between dealers on the basis of quotations published in commercial "sheets" by broker-dealers who chose to make markets in particular securities. However, in 1971, the NASD put into operation an electronic automated quotation system (NASDAQ) for selected OTC securities, in which dealers can insert, and instantaneously update, bid and asked quotations for securities in which they are registered with the NASD as market makers. The NASD thus now combines the dual functions of an exchange: regulating access to and operation of NASDAQ, and regulating the internal affairs of those of its members which are not members of any exchange (generally the smaller firms.)

A firm is not required to join the NASD in order to trade in OTC securities. However, SEA § 15A(e)(1) provides that an association may bar its members from giving a "dealer discount" to a non-member, and the NASD rule to that effect makes it an economic necessity for any dealer which wants to participate in offerings underwritten by NASD members to join the NASD. In 1964, Congress became concerned with the lack of regulation over firms which chose not to join the NASD, and considered requiring all broker-dealers to become members. However, it opted instead for an extension of SEC authority, empowering the Commission to establish standards for training and experience of personnel and other rules governing the conduct of non-members of the NASD, comparable to those which the NASD applies to its own members. See SEA § 15(b)(7)–(9), Rules 15b10–1 *et seq.*

Securities Acts Amendments of 1975. Between 1968 and 1970, the securities industry passed through an operational and financial crisis which ultimately led to extensive Congressional modification of the self-regulatory scheme. The Securities Acts Amendments of 1975 made important changes in the powers of the SRO's and the SEC's role in supervising them.

SEA § 19, as amended in 1975, expanded and consolidated the SEC's authority over *all* self-regulatory organizations. The SEC's new authority with respect to exchanges and the NASD is roughly comparable to, but even broader than, its previous authority over the NASD. In particular, the SEC must now give advance approval for any exchange rule changes, and has review power over exchange disciplinary actions. The 1975 amendments also confirmed the SEC action terminating the power of exchanges to fix minimum rates of commission (which both Congress and the SEC found to have been a major cause of market distortion) and directed the SEC to eliminate any other exchange rules which imposed unwarranted restraints on competition.

(a) Civil Liability Under SRO Rules

In addition to the questions of policy discussed above, the authority delegated by Congress to non-governmental entities to adopt rules having the force of law has given rise to two difficult questions of civil liability. The first question is whether a self-regulatory organization can be held liable in damages for failure to enforce its rules. The second question is whether a customer of a broker-dealer has an implied private right of action against the firm for damages resulting from its violation of an exchange or NASD rule, as he has in the case of violation of an SEC rule.

Exchange or NASD Liability. While an exchange probably cannot be held liable for failing to *adopt* a rule which would have prevented injury to a plaintiff, see Cutner v. Fried, 373 F.Supp.

4 (S.D.N.Y.1974), it can be held liable for damages resulting from its failure to *enforce* a rule which it has adopted. In Baird v. Franklin, 141 F.2d 238 (2d Cir. 1944), the court held that SEA § 6(b), under which the rules of an exchange must provide for appropriate sanctions against members who engage in conduct inconsistent with just and equitable principles of trade, "places a duty upon the Stock Exchange to enforce the rules and regulations prescribed by that section" (that duty is now explicitly imposed by SEA § 19(g)(1), added in 1975).

Thus, if an exchange knows or has reason to know that a member is in violation of one of its rules and fails to take appropriate action, it may be held liable to a person who suffers damages as a result of such inaction. Yet, despite this clear statement of the basis for liability, there is as yet no reported case in which an exchange has actually been required to pay damages for failure to enforce its rules. In each case, the court has held either that there was no violation, see Kroese v. NYSE, 227 F.Supp. 519 (S.D.N.Y. 1964), or that the exchange had no reason to know of it, see Butterman v. Walston & Co., 387 F.2d 822 (7th Cir. 1967), or that the action taken by the exchange was reasonable under the circumstances, see Hughes v. Dempsey-Tegeler & Co., 534 F.2d 156 (9th Cir. 1976), or, as in *Baird* itself, that the failure to act did not cause the plaintiff's loss because the assets had all been dissipated before the exchange found out about the violation.

While claims of customers of NYSE member firms that failed during the 1968–70 financial crisis were paid out of the NYSE's "trust fund", a number of actions were instituted against the exchange by investors in those firms, alleging that their losses had been caused by the exchange's failure to enforce its "net capital" rules. In the first appellate court decision on the question, the Ninth Circuit held that an investor had standing to bring such an action, but then denied recovery on other grounds. Hughes v. Dempsey-Tegeler, *supra*. In subsequent decisions, however, the Second Circuit held that, since SEA § 6 was enacted for the benefit of public investors, an action for damages under that section can be brought only by members of that class. It accordingly held that an action could not be brought by the receiver of a bankrupt firm, Lank v. NYSE, 548 F.2d 61 (2d Cir. 1977), or by "those who invest in a member of a securities exchange, whether as limited partners, subordinated lenders, or purchasers of other than its publicly traded securities," Arneil v. Ramsey, 550 F.2d 774 (2d Cir. 1977). The same court has also held that an exchange has no obligation to convey information in its possession to potential investors in a firm, and that it cannot be held liable for "aiding and abetting" a fraud practised by the firm on investors unless it knew of the fraud or actively participated in it. Hirsch v. du Pont, 553 F.2d 750 (2d Cir. 1977); Murphy v. McDonnell & Co., 553 F.2d 292 (2d Cir. 1977).

Liability for Violation of Rule. The other question is whether an SRO member who violates one of the rules of the organization is liable in damages to a person injured by the violation. In Colonial Realty Corp. v. Bache & Co., 358 F.2d 178 (2d Cir. 1966), the court declined to hold either that there would always be, or that there would never be, a private right of action for violation of an exchange or NASD rule. The question, said Judge Friendly, was "the nature of the particular rule and its place in the regulatory scheme." The case for implying a private right of action would be strongest where a rule "provides what amounts to a substitute for regulation by the SEC itself" and "imposes an explicit duty unknown to the common law"; it would be weakest in a case, like *Colonial,* where plaintiff was claiming that failure to comply with an alleged oral understanding violated the exchange's "catch-all" prohibition against "conduct inconsistent with just and equitable principles of trade."

This distinction has proved difficult to apply in practice. In Buttrey v. Merrill Lynch, 410 F.2d 135 (7th Cir. 1969), the court held that a broker, which failed to make adequate inquiry as to the source of the securities which a customer was trading, could be held liable to the persons from whom the securities were fraudulently converted on the basis of a violation of the NYSE's "know your customer" rule, where the broker's conduct was "tantamount to fraud." Another court, however, following the *Colonial* approach, has held that there should never be a private right of action under the "know your customer" rule, because it was "enacted primarily for the protection of the dealers." Nelson v. Hench, 428 F.Supp. 411 (D.Minn.1977). In Mercury Investment Co. v. A. G. Edwards, 295 F.Supp. 1160 (S.D.Tex. 1969), the court held that a violation of the NASD's "suitability" rule would not give rise to civil liability, even though it was a specific rule obviously intended for the protection of the customer; it was simply too far removed from the type of *fraudulent* activity at which the securities laws were directed. The court did say, however, that violation of the rule would be admissible as evidence of negligence in plaintiff's common law claim.

A review of these cases leads to the conclusion that the availability of a private right of action may depend more on the seriousness of the defendant's violation than on the place of the particular rule in the regulatory spectrum.

(b) Antitrust Limitations on SRO Actions

As noted above, an SRO may be held civilly liable for failure to enforce its rules. On the other hand, it may also be held civilly liable for action taken to enforce those rules, if a member or non-member injured by the action can show that the SRO lacked legal authority for the action it took.

Prior to the 1975 amendments, there was no statutory means of obtaining SEC or court review of an exchange disciplinary action (NASD disciplinary actions were subject to SEC review). The principal vehicle for attacking exchange actions in the courts, therefore, was federal antitrust law, particularly the prohibition in § 1 of the Sherman Act against "contracts, combinations or conspiracies in restraint of trade." The theory of such attacks was that, since an exchange is an association of competing broker-dealers, any action it takes which limits the ability of members to compete with one another, or the ability of non-members to compete with members, is a *per se* violation of the Sherman Act, unless the exchange is exempted from the antitrust laws by the provisions of the federal securities laws.

Silver v. NYSE, 373 U.S. 341 (1963), involved an NYSE order to its members to terminate their wire connections with plaintiff, a broker-dealer who dealt solely in unlisted securities. The district court held that the NYSE action was a *per se* violation of the antitrust laws, since the NYSE had no statutory power to regulate trading in unlisted securities. The court of appeals reversed, holding that the NYSE had statutory power to regulate all transactions by its members, including their transactions in unlisted securities, and that since the NYSE action was "within the general scope of its authority" under the 1934 Act, that action was exempt from the antitrust laws. The Supreme Court rejected both extremes. It held that the NYSE did have statutory authority to regulate its members' transactions in unlisted securities, but that the 1934 Act did not automatically repeal the antitrust laws with respect to any action which the Exchange had authority to take. "Repeal is to be regarded as implied only if necessary to make the [Act] work, and even then only to the minimum extent necessary. This is the guiding principal to reconciliation of the [antitrust laws and securities laws]."

With respect to the specific situation before it, the Court said that since the SEC had no power to review Exchange disciplinary actions, there was "nothing built into the regulatory scheme which performs the antitrust function of insuring that an exchange will not in some cases apply its rules so as to do injury to competition which cannot be justified as furthering legitimate self-regulative ends." And since the NYSE had refused to tell the plaintiff the nature of the charges against him or afford him an opportunity to explain or refute them, the NYSE had no basis for justifying its action in that case as "necessary to make the Exchange Act work."

This "antitrust-due process" approach has been followed in a number of subsequent cases, see, e. g., Zuckerman v. Yount, 362 F.Supp. 858 (N.D. Ill.1973), and also held applicable to the NASD. Harwell v. Growth Programs, Inc., 451 F.2d 240 (5th Cir. 1971). However, the need to resort to antitrust law to attack SRO disciplinary actions is substantially lessened by SEA § 19(d), added in 1975, which makes all SRO disciplinary actions reviewable by the SEC (and thus ultimately by the courts.)

The more significant question raised by the decisions in *Silver* was whether the antitrust laws applied to exchange *rules* which operated to restrict competition, particularly the exchange rules which required members to charge fixed minimum rates of commission on all transactions. This situation was distinguishable from *Silver*, since the SEC had explicit statutory power to order changes in exchange rules governing commission rates. However, in 1970, the Seventh Circuit, finding "no evidence that the SEC is exercising actual and adequate review jurisdiction" over commission rates, held that the mere possibility of SEC review did not immunize the rules from antitrust attack, and that the exchange had the burden of showing that such rules were "necessary to make the Exchange Act work." Thill Securities Corp. v. NYSE, 433 F.2d 264 (7th Cir. 1970).

Finally, in 1975, *after* the SEC had ordered an end to fixed commission rates and *after* Congress had confirmed that decision in the 1975 amendments, the Supreme Court held that the pre-existing rules fixing commission rates were not subject to antitrust attack. The Court said that, "given the expertise of the SEC, the confidence the Congress has placed in the agency, and the active roles the SEC and the Congress have taken, permitting courts throughout the country to conduct their own antitrust proceedings would conflict with the regulatory scheme authorized by Congress." Gordon v. NYSE, 422 U.S. 659 (1975).

Since the 1975 Amendments confirm the termination of fixed commission rates, and direct the SEC to "review existing and proposed rules of the self-regulatory organizations and to abrogate any present rule or to disapprove any proposed rule imposing a competitive restraint neither necessary nor appropriate in furtherance of a legitimate regulatory objective," H.Rep. No. 94–229, at 94 (1975), future application of antitrust laws and principles to exchange and NASD actions will most likely arise in the course of SEC review of those actions, rather than in separate proceedings in the courts.

VI. REGULATION OF INVEST-MENT COMPANIES

In § 30 of the Public Utility Holding Company Act of 1935, Congress directed the SEC to make a study of investment trusts and investment companies, their corporate structure, their investment policies, and their influence on the companies in which they invest. The resulting SEC study, submitted to Congress in 1938–39, detailed a number of serious abuses in the operation of these investment vehicles. It led to the passage of the Investment Company Act of 1940 (ICA), which provided for SEC regulation of investment company activities.

Following World War II, investment companies (particularly mutual funds) experienced a period of rapid growth. A Wharton School "Study of Mutual Funds" (1962) for the SEC, and the SEC's own report on "Public Policy Implications of Investment Company Growth" (1966) suggested the need for modification of the 1940 Act, particularly with respect to the controls over management and sales compensation. After four years of hearings, reflecting serious disagreements between the SEC and the industry, Congress passed the Investment Company Act Amendments of 1970, significantly revising the law. Further minor changes were made in the Securities Acts Amendments of 1975.

§ 26. Coverage of the 1940 Act

The Investment Company Act (i) requires every investment company to register with the SEC, (ii) imposes substantive restrictions on the activities of a registered investment company and persons connected with it, and (iii) provides for a variety of SEC and private sanctions.

Under ICA § 3(a), an investment company is an entity which (a) is * * * engaged *primarily* * * * in the business of investing, reinvesting or trading in securities," or (b) is "engaged" in that business and more than 40% of its assets consist of "investment securities" (i. e., all securities other than government securities and securities of majority-owned subsidiaries).

(a) Types of Investment Companies

Most investment companies are organized as corporations, although they may also be set up in trust, partnership or other forms. Most of the regulatory provisions use corporate terms such as "directors" and "shareholders", so that appropriate modifications must be made when other forms are used.

The Act divides investment companies into three classes: "face-amount certificate companies", which issue fixed-income debenture-type securities; "unit investment trusts", which offer interests in a fixed portfolio of securities, and the most important class, "management companies," which includes all other types of investment companies. ICA § 4.

"Management companies" are further divided into "open-end" and "closed-end" companies, ICA § 5(a), and into "diversified" and "non-diversified" companies, ICA § (5b). "Open-end companies", commonly known as "mutual funds," are those which offer redeemable securities. They generally offer shares on a continuous basis, at a price related to current net asset value (i. e., the current market value of the fund's portfolio divided by the number of shares of the fund outstanding), and stand ready to redeem shares at any time at the shareholder's request, also at net asset value or at a price related to it. "Closed-end companies" are more similar to other types of corporations; at any time, they have a fixed number of shares outstanding, which are traded either on an exchange or in the over-the-counter market, at prices which reflect supply and demand and may be substantially above or below the net asset value.

An investment company is "diversified" if, with respect to at least 75% of its portfolio the securities of any single issuer do not account for (a) more than 5% of the investment company's assets, or (b) more than 10% of the outstanding voting securities of that issuer. (These diversification requirements are similar to those which permit an investment company to qualify for special tax treatment under § 851(b)(4) of the Internal Revenue Code.)   Since diversification depends on the amount of investment in a single issuer, an investment company which invests solely in a single industry or geographical area is still considered "diversified."

(b) Exemptions

"Inadvertent" Investment Companies.   Because of the broad definition of "investment company" in ICA § 3(a), an operating company which sells a significant part of its assets and reinvests the proceeds in securities of other companies which it does not control may find itself in the position of an "inadvertent" investment company, subject to serious restrictions on its activities if it registers with the SEC, or to severe sanctions if it does not.   Compounding this dilemma in many cases is the difficulty of determining what the company's "principal" business is, or how to value its "investment securities" and other assets for the purpose of determining whether it meets the 40% test.   See SEC v. Fifth Ave. Coach Lines, 289 F. Supp. 3 (S.D.N.Y.1968).

Even if more than 40% of a company's assets are "investment securities", it is not considered an investment company if either (i) it is primarily engaged in other businesses, directly or through wholly-owned subsidiaries, or (ii) it applies for and obtains an SEC order declaring it to be primarily engaged in other businesses, directly or through majority-owned subsidiaries, or through "controlled companies conducting similar types of businesses." ICA §§ 3(b)(1), (2). While the former exemption is self-executing, the latter provides a broader exemption where the company can convince the SEC that its relationships with its "controlled companies" take it outside the purposes of the Act.

Closely-held Companies. ICA § 3(c)(1) excludes from the definition of "investment company" any issuer which has not more than 100 beneficial security holders and which is not making any public offering of securities. Relying on this exemption, a large number of private "hedge funds" were established during the 1960s, usually in partnership form, to engage in short selling, margin transactions, option trading, and other types of aggressive investment practices barred to registered investment companies.

Specialized Investment Media. The Act excludes from coverage banks, insurance companies, savings and loan associations, finance companies, oil and gas drilling funds, charitable foundations, tax-exempt pension funds, and other special types of institutions. ICA §§ 3(c)(3)–(13). However, insurance companies and banks have been held to be subject to the Act when they publicly offer investment plans or services in which the rate of return varies depending on the performance of a separate fund of securities.

In Prudential Insurance Co. v. SEC, 326 F.2d 383 (3d Cir. 1964), the court accepted the SEC position that a separate account established by an insurance company to fund "variable annuities" was itself an investment company required to register under the Act, even though the company which operated the account was clearly engaged primarily in the business of insurance. The 1970 amendments subsequently exempted separate accounts used to fund certain types of employee pension plans. ICA § 3(c)(11). When insurance companies began to develop "variable life insurance" in the early 1970's, the SEC first took the position that the separate accounts used to fund such insurance should be exempt from the Act because of the possible conflicts with state insurance laws. ICA Rel. 7644 (1973). However, the SEC subsequently reversed this position, withdrew the blanket exemption, and adopted new rules to exempt such accounts only from specified provisions of the Act. ICA Rel. 9482 (1976).

Common trust funds, and collective funds maintained by banks for investment of pension fund assets, are specifically excluded from the definition of "investment company." ICA §§ 3(c)(3), (11). In 1962, the Comptroller of the Currency authorized national banks to establish commingled funds for "managing agency accounts," in effect permitting them to offer their customers interests in a bank-managed "mutual fund." After unsuccessful efforts by the banking industry to have such funds exempted from the securities laws, one bank registered its account with the SEC as an investment company, obtaining an exemption from ICA § 10(c), which bars an investment company from having a majority of its directors affiliated with any one bank. The granting of this exemption by the SEC was upheld on appeal. NASD v. SEC, 420 F.2d 83 (D. C.Cir. 1969). However, the Supreme Court subsequently mooted the question by ruling that a bank's operation of such a fund involved "underwriting" of securities in violation of the Glass-Steagall Act. Investment Company Institute v. Camp, 401 U.S. 617 (1971).

§ 27. Regulation of Fund Activities

Registration and Reporting Requirements. An investment company registers with the SEC by filing a notification of registration setting forth a statement of its investment policy and other specified information, ICA § 10. A registered company must file annual reports with the Commission, ICA § 30, and maintain specified accounts and records, ICA § 31.

Protection of Assets. As a safeguard against looting of investment company assets, all securities must be held in the custody of a bank or stock exchange member, or under strict procedures laid down by the SEC. ICA § 17(f), Rule

17f–2. Larceny or embezzlement from an investment company is a federal crime, ICA § 37, and officers and employees who have access to the company's cash or securities must be bonded. ICA § 17(g), Rule 17g–1.

Capital Structure. An open-end company (mutual fund) may not issue any "senior security" (debt or preferred stock) other than notes to evidence bank borrowings. ICA § 18(f). A closed-end company may issue not more than one class of debt securities and not more than one class of preferred stock, provided that it has an asset coverage of at least 300 percent, in the case of debt, or 200 percent, in the case of preferred stock. ICA §§ 18(a), (c). No registered management company may issue any rights or warrants to purchase any of its securities. ICA § 18(d). An investment company may not make any public offering of its securities until it has a net worth of at least $100,000. ICA § 14(a).

Dividends. No dividends may be paid from any source other than accumulated undistributed net income, or net income for the current or preceding fiscal year, unless accompanied by a written statement disclosing the source of such payment. Under the tax laws, an investment company must pay dividends to its shareholders amounting to at least 90 percent of its taxable ordinary income each year to avoid double taxation of its income to itself and its shareholders. IRC § 852(a)(1).

Investment Activities. An investment company may not purchase securities on margin, sell short, or participate in joint trading accounts. ICA § 12(a). It may not incur underwriting commitments aggregating more than 25% of the value of its total assets. ICA § 12(c). Unless authorized by the vote of the holders of a majority of its voting securities, it may not borrow money, issue senior securities, underwrite any securities, purchase or sell real estate or commodities, make loans, change its investment policy with respect to concentration or diversification, change its subclassification, or change the nature of its business so as to cease to be an investment company. ICA § 13(a).

Investment companies, unlike trusts, insurance companies and other types of institutional investors, are not limited to a "legal list" in making investments, nor are they subject to the "prudent man" rule. The managers, therefore, cannot be held liable for losses resulting from investments which turned out badly or might have been deemed "imprudent" by a conservative investor. The managers are subject to SEC sanctions, however, if they fail to provide the kind of investment management and supervision which they have advertised in their sales literature or statements of policy. Managed Funds, SA Rel. 4122 (1959); Financial Programs, SEA Rel. 11312 (1975); Chase Investment Services, IAA Rel. 449

(1975). In such situations, the directors of the fund may also be held civilly liable, under state law, for damages caused by the mismanagement. Lutz v. Boas, 171 A.2d 381 (Del.Ch.1961). In Brouk v. Managed Funds, 286 F.2d 901 (8th Cir. 1961), the court held that such mismanagement did not give rise to an implied right of action against the directors under the Investment Company Act, but that holding has been discredited by other decisions. See e. g., Brown v. Bullock, 294 F.2d 415 (2d Cir. 1961).

Fund Investments in Other Funds. As a result of its unpleasant experience in the 1960's with The Fund of Funds, a large European-based mutual fund which invested heavily in the shares of American mutual funds, the SEC urged Congress to prohibit any investment company from acquiring shares of any other investment company. The 1970 amendments, however, did not impose a complete prohibition. Instead, they limited such investment so that no investment company can own more than 3% of the stock of another investment company nor invest more than 5% of its assets in any one investment company or more than 10% of its assets in other investment companies generally. ICA § 12(d).

§ 28. Management and Control

(a) Shareholders, Directors and Officers

All shares of stock issued by an investment company must have equal voting rights, and voting trusts are prohibited, ICA §§ 18(i), 20(b). Solicitations of proxies from investment company shareholders are subject to approximately the same rules that apply under SEA § 14 to solicitations of shareholders of listed companies. ICA § 20(a), Rules 20a–1, 2, 3.

In addition to their voting rights under the laws of an investment company's state of incorporation, shareholders are entitled to vote on: changes in investment policy or status, ICA § 13(a), approval or assignment of investment advisory contracts, ICA § 15(a), filling of more than a specified number of vacancies in the board of directors, ICA § 16(a), sale of stock of a closed-end company below net asset value, ICA § 23(b), and appointment of independent public accountants, ICA § 32(a).

The Act contains a number of provisions designed to insure the integrity of directors and officers and the independence of the board of directors. Under ICA § 9(a), no person who has been convicted within 10 years of a securities-related felony or is enjoined from securities-related activities may serve as a director or officer or in certain other specified capacities. And ICA § 17(b) prohibits any provisions indemnifying directors or officers against liabilities to the company arising out of their willful misfeasance, bad faith, gross negligence or reckless disregard of duty.

To assure the existence of independent voices on the board of directors, ICA § 10(a) provides that no more than 60% of the members of the board may be "interested persons" of the company. (There is an exception for "no-load" funds managed by registered investment advisers, which are required to have only one "non-interested" director. ICA § 10(d).) The term "interested person" was introduced by the 1970 amendments, and represents a significant broadening of the category of "affiliated persons" which was the standard prior to 1970. In addition to "affiliated persons", who are persons in a direct control relationship with the investment company or its adviser, ICA § 2(a)(3), the term "interested person" includes any broker-dealer or affiliate of a broker-dealer, any person who has served as legal counsel to the company within the past two years, any member of the immediate family of an affiliated person, and any other person whom the SEC determines to have had "a material business or professional relationship" with the company or its principal executive officer within the past two years. ICA § 2(a)(19).

(b) Management Compensation

In contrast to most business corporations, which are managed by their own officers, acting under the supervision of the board of directors, investment companies, particularly mutual funds, normally contract with a separate entity known as the "investment adviser" to provide all management and advisory services to the investment company for a fee. In fact, the normal procedure is for the investment advisory organization (which may be a partnership or a privately or publicly held corporation) to create one or more mutual funds as "corporate shells" to serve as vehicles for pooling the investments of a large number of small customers.

In an effort to protect the shareholders of an investment company from overreaching by the adviser, ICA § 15(a) provides that an investment adviser must serve under a written contract approved initially by a vote of the shareholders and thereafter approved annually by the board of directors of the investment company.

The typical investment advisory contract calls for compensation of the adviser on the basis of a percentage of the fund's net assets. As mutual funds developed, the most common arrangement was to set the annual advisory or management fee at ½ of 1% of the average net assets of the fund during the year. As some funds grew in size during the 1950's to $1 billion or more, the annual fees charged by their advisers increased correspondingly to $5 million or more a year. Critics of the industry, subsequently joined by the SEC, attacked these fees on the grounds that they bore no relation to the value of the services provided by the adviser, and were grossly out of line with fees charged for the management of pension funds and other portfolios of comparable size and investment objectives. Derivative suits were brought by shareholders on behalf of a number of funds alleging that the high fees constituted a waste of corporate assets and a breach of the directors' fiduciary duties to the funds under state corporation law and the Investment Company Act. In the fully litigated cases, the plaintiffs were unsuccessful. The courts, while finding the fees "high", held that they were not so "unconscionable" or "shocking" as to constitute "waste." Acampora v. Birkland, 220 F.Supp. 527 (D.Colo.1963); Saxe v. Brady, 40 Del.Ch. 474, 184 A.2d 602 (1962); Meiselman v. Eberstadt, 39 Del.Ch. 563, 170 A.2d 720 (1961). However, a number of other cases were settled, with the adviser agreeing to scale down the fee to a lower percentage of assets as the fund reached a certain size, or making other adjustments.

In its 1966 report to Congress on mutual funds, the SEC recommended that the Act be amended to subject advisory fees to a statutory standard of "reasonableness", with a listing of factors to be taken into account in determining whether a particular fee was "reasonable." The industry vehemently opposed this recommendation, and the 1970 amendments to the act took a different approach. A new provision was added to ICA § 36, under which an investment adviser is "deemed to have a fiduciary duty with respect to the receipt of compensation for services" from an investment company. This duty is specifically made enforcible in the courts, either by the SEC or in a derivative suit by a fund shareholder. While the Congressional reports on this amendment refer to the developments which led up to the legislation, they do not define the content of the adviser's "fiduciary duty," and the paucity of subsequent litigation makes it difficult to say precisely what that duty is. It has been held, however, to bar an adviser from increasing its fees, even with shareholder approval, where the increase was of no benefit to the investment company. See Galfand v. Chestnutt, 545 F.2d 807 (2d Cir. 1976).

As an additional measure to assure adequate consideration of advisory fees by an investment company's board of directors, the 1970 amendments also added ICA § 15(c), under which any amendment or renewal of the advisory contract must be approved by a majority of the *disinterested* directors, who are under a duty to request "such information as may reasonably be necessary to evaluate the terms of [the] contract."

(c) Transfer of Management

One of the evils at which the 1940 Act was aimed was "trafficking" in advisory contracts, in which the adviser to an investment company would assign its rights under the contract to another person or entity. Accordingly, ICA § 15(a)(4) required that every advisory contract with an investment company automatically terminate upon its assignment. The term "assignment" was defined to include any transfer of a controlling interest in the management organization, ICA § 2(a)(4), so that any such transfer would also require approval by the shareholders of the investment company.

In SEC v. Insurance Securities, 254 F.2d 642 (9th Cir. 1958), the Commission sought to enjoin the sale of stock in a management organization at a substantial premium above its book value as a "gross abuse of trust" in violation of ICA § 36, even though it was approved by the fund's shareholders. The Commission argued that the capitalized value of the expected future earnings from the advisory contract represented an asset of the fund, which the adviser or its shareholders could not appropriate. The court rejected the SEC contention, holding that the expectation of future earnings was an element of the adviser's business which it could transfer for a profit.

In its 1966 report, the SEC proposed the addition of a provision to the Act which would bar transfer of control of a management organization where it was "likely to impose additional burdens on the investment company or to limit its freedom of future action." In view of uncertainty as to the purpose and scope of this recommendation, no such provision was added in the 1970 amendments. However, in Rosenfeld v. Black, 445 F.2d 1337 (2d Cir. 1971), a shareholder's derivative action attacking the payment of a fee to the former adviser in connection with a change of advisers, the court adopted the position originally urged by the SEC in the *Insurance Securities* case, and held that the transaction, under the circumstances presented, was a breach of the adviser's implied fiduciary duty under the ICA. This decision created great uncertainty as to when, if ever, the stock of a management organization could be sold at a premium over net asset value. Congress therefore added a new § 15(f) to the ICA in 1975, providing that no attack could be made on the amount received on such a sale, provided that (a) for a period of three years after the sale, at least 75% of the directors of the investment company must be disinterested (instead of the normal 40%), and (b) no unfair burdens (in the form of compensation for anything other than bona fide services) are imposed on the investment company as a result of the transaction.

§ 29. Transactions with Affiliates

One obvious possibility for abuse by the persons in control of an investment company is to cause the investment company to buy securities from them, or to sell securities to them, at a price which is more favorable to them than to the investment company. Under ICA § 17(a), therefore, it is illegal for any affiliated person, promoter or principal underwriter of an investment company to sell securities or other property to the company, or buy them from the company, or to borrow from the company, subject to certain limited exceptions. However, under ICA § 17(b), the SEC is authorized, upon application, to exempt a proposed transaction from the prohibition of § 17(a) if it finds that the transaction (1) is fair and reasonable and does not involve overreaching on the part of any person concerned, (2) is consistent with the policy of the investment company, and (3) is consistent with the general purposes of the Act. Under this standard, the SEC must be satisfied that the transaction is fair, not only to the investment company, but to all other parties to the transaction. E. I. duPont & Co. v. Collins, 97 S.Ct. 2229 (1977).

(a) Joint Transactions

In addition to the prohibition on transactions between an investment company and an affiliate, ICA § 17(d) bars affiliates and underwriters from entering into any transaction in which the investment company is a "joint participant", in contravention of SEC rules designed to prevent the investment company from participating "on a basis different from or less advantageous than" the other participant. Under the authority of this section, the SEC has adopted Rule 17d–1, requiring all joint arrangements to be approved by the Commission before any transactions are consummated. A pattern or practice under which officers or directors repeatedly make investments in enterprises in which the investment company is also investing has been held to be a "joint arrangement" within the meaning of these provisions. SEC v. Midwest Tech. Devel. Corp., CCH ¶ 91,252 (D.Minn.1963).

The "Portfolio Affiliate" Problem. The term "affiliated person", as defined in ICA § 2(a)(3), includes not only any person who "controls" an investment company or owns more than 5% of its stock, but also any corporation or other entity more than 5% of the stock of which is owned by the investment company. Any understanding between an investment company and one of these "portfolio affiliates" (for example, with respect to acquiring substantial interests in the stock of another corporation in connection with a takeover bid) may constitute a "joint arrangement" requiring SEC approval. SEC v. Talley Industries, 399 F.2d 396 (2d Cir. 1968).

(b) Brokerage Transactions

ICA § 17(e) bars an affiliated person from receiving any compensation for acting as an agent or broker in any transaction by the investment company, except that such a person may receive a brokerage commission for effecting securities transactions for the investment company, provided it does not exceed "the usual and customary broker's commission" for such transactions. This exception permits brokerage firms which act as advisers to investment companies also to act as brokers for those companies. However, the elimination of fixed minimum commissions on stock exchange transactions in 1975 (see § 25(b) *supra*) complicates the problem of determining when a commission exceeds the "usual and customary commission."

The most difficult problem with respect to brokerage commissions, however, has not been the direct payment of commissions to affiliated brokers, but the routing of commissions to brokerage firms which provided other services to the investment company or its adviser. Prior to 1975, the rules of the various stock exchanges specified minimum commissions to be paid on all transactions. Investment companies tend to trade in larger-than-average transactions which, under the existing commission rate schedules, were highly profitable to the brokerage firms which executed them. Investment company managers therefore began to direct their brokerage business to firms which also performed other services, particularly those which sold mutual fund shares to the public, thus increasing the size of the fund and consequently the fee received by the adviser. Under stock exchange rules, it was not necessary to direct the actual orders to the firms which sold fund shares; a large order could be directed to a firm skilled in executing such orders, with instructions to "give up" a portion of the commission (often as much as 75%) to other firms which sold fund shares.

Managers of investment companies which had no use for these "give-ups" (because they did not sell shares to the public through broker-dealers) then discovered that, by establishing brokerage affiliates and having them become members of regional stock exchanges, they could recapture through "give-ups" a large part of the commissions paid on their portfolio transactions. The benefits of the "recapture" could then be passed on to the investment company by means of a corresponding reduction in the management fee. As these practices became publicly known, shareholders of a number of investment companies brought derivative suits against the "affiliated" directors of the investment companies, alleging that their failure to bring the possibility of recapture to the attention of the "unaffiliated" directors was a breach of their fiduciary duty under ICA § 36. Courts of Appeals in two circuits have upheld the imposition of liability in these circumstances. Moses v. Burgin, 445 F.2d 369 (1st Cir. 1971); Fogel v. Chestnutt, 533 F.2d 731 (2d Cir. 1975). However, the "affiliated" directors cannot be held liable for failure to effect a recapture of commissions if the relevant facts and considerations were fully disclosed to the unaffiliated directors and the shareholders. Tannenbaum v. Zeller, 552 F.2d 402 (2d Cir. 1977).

The termination of fixed commission rates in 1975 substantially eliminated the "give-up" problem. However, in the 1975 Securities Acts Amendments, Congress added a new § 28(e) to the Securities Exchange Act, under which an adviser to an investment company or any other institution is deemed not to have breached any fiduciary duty under state or federal law by causing the institution to pay a broker a higher commission than other brokers would charge for the same transaction if the adviser determines in good faith that the commission is reasonable "in relation to the value of the brokerage and research services" provided by the broker to all accounts under the adviser's management. This provision for "paying up for research", designed to assure the survival of research-oriented brokerage firms, reintroduces, although in more limited form, the conflicts of interest between investment company and adviser that characterized the fixed commission rate system.

§ 30. Sale of Fund Shares

As noted above, investment companies are divided into "closed-end" and "open-end" companies. Closed-end companies, like other corporations, issue a fixed number of shares to the public in a one-shot underwritten offering. Open-end companies, or "mutual funds", make a continuous offering of shares at a price related to the current "net asset value" (i. e., the current market value of the fund's portfolio, divided by the number of shares outstanding). Mutual funds are in turn divided into "load" and "no-load" funds. Load funds distribute their shares to the public either through securities dealers or (in the case of a few large fund complexes) through their own "captive" sales forces, charging a sales commission, or "load", ranging up to $8\frac{1}{2}\%$ of the public offering price. No-load funds sell shares directly to the public through the mail, charging the current net asset value, with no sales charge added. The principal underwriter of a fund's shares must operate under a written contract renewed at least annually by the shareholders or directors of the fund, ICA § 15(b).

(a) Disclosure Requirements

The disclosure requirements of the Securities Act of 1933 apply to investment companies, but with certain modifications. Under ICA § 24(a), an investment company's registration statement, instead of containing the information required by Schedule A to the 1933 Act, may set forth certain of the information contained in the company's reports under ICA § 30. And ICA § 24(b) requires that any sales literature used by a mutual fund to supplement the information contained in its prospectus must be filed with the SEC. In addition, since mutual funds make continuous offerings of their shares, ICA § 24(e)(3) modifies SA §§ 11 and 13 to provide that the effective date of the most recent amendment to a fund's registration statement is deemed to be the effective date of the registration statement and the date of commencement of the fund's public offering. (In the absence of this provision, people who purchased fund shares several years after the commencement of the fund's public offering would have no right of action under SA §§ 11 and 12.)

The SEC has been strongly criticized for using its authority over supplementary sales literature to impose unduly strict limitations on what mutual funds can say in their advertising. In 1974, the Commission accordingly amended SA Rule 134 to "allow more interesting and informative mutual fund advertisements," and also revised its "Statement of Policy" on investment company sales literature to permit new methods of portraying the total return on an investment in the fund. See ICA Rels. 8568, 8571.

(b) Controls on Prices

Closed-End Companies. To prevent "dilution" of the interests of existing shareholders, ICA § 23(b) prohibits closed-end companies from issuing shares at a price below their current net asset value without the consent of a majority of their shareholders. Since the shares of closed-end companies normally trade in the market at substantial discounts from net asset value, this provision makes it extremely difficult for existing closed-end companies to make additional offerings of their shares.

Open-End Companies. ICA § 22 contains a complicated set of provisions governing the prices at which shares of open-end companies, or "mutual funds" can be sold to the public. ICA § 22(a) authorizes the NASD to adopt rules prescribing the methods of computing the price at which its members may purchase shares from the fund and resell them to the public, for the purpose of preventing dilution or unfair discrimination between different purchasers or holders of fund shares.

ICA § 22(d) provides that no fund shares may be sold to the public "except at a current offering price described in the prospectus." If a particular fund states in its prospectus that its shares are offered at current net asset value plus a sales load of 8½%, no dealer may sell shares of that fund to the public at any other price. The price-fixing provisions of § 22(d), like other "retail price maintenance" statutes, have been defended by the industry on the ground that they are essential to the maintenance of an "orderly distribution system." In its 1966 Mutual Fund Report to Congress, the SEC pointed out how the statutory restraint on competition had produced uneconomically high sales charges for mutual fund shares, but stopped short of recommending that § 22(d) be repealed. Instead, it persuaded Congress to modify ICA § 22(b) (which had previously contained a prohibition against "unconscionable or grossly excessive" sales loads) to give the NASD authority to fix maximum sales loads so that the public offering price "shall not include an excessive sales load but shall allow for reasonable compensation for sales personnel, broker-dealers, and underwriters, and for reasonable sales loads to investors." The NASD, operating under this "reasonable" standard, eventually adopted rules, effective June 1, 1976, under which sales loads may not exceed 8½% (the previously prevailing figure).

Mutual funds generally offer a "volume discount", under which purchasers of large amounts of shares pay a lower percentage sales load. The question arose, therefore, whether a number of purchasers (e. g., members of a professional association) could aggregate their purchases as a group to take advantage of the volume discounts. In 1958, the SEC, in response to industry concerns that group discounts would also impair the "orderly distribution system", adopted ICA Rule 22d–1, barring dealers from offering the same volume discounts to a group of small investors that they could offer to a single large investor. In 1974, however, responding to pressures for some opportunity for price competition, the Commission amended Rule 22d–1 to permit the extension of volume discounts to certain "bona fide" groups of employees, association members, and the like.

Another possible avenue of competition in sales charges for mutual fund shares would be the development of a "secondary" market, in which brokers could sell and purchase already outstanding mutual fund shares for their customers, at a price between net asset value and net asset value plus sales load.   In U. S. v. NASD, 422 U.S. 694 (1975), the Justice Department charged that mutual fund sponsors, securities broker-dealers, and the NASD had violated the antitrust laws by conspiring to prevent the development of such a secondary market.   The defendants argued that ICA § 22 was intended to exempt the distribution of mutual fund shares from the operation of the antitrust laws.   The Supreme Court, in a 5–4 decision, agreed with their contention.   While it held that § 22(d), which controls the price at which *dealers* can sell mutual fund shares, did not apply to sales by investors through securities firms acting as *brokers*, it went on to hold that § 22(f), which authorizes mutual funds to restrict the negotiability and transferability of their shares, did authorize the kind of restrictive arrangements which the Justice Department was attacking.

Contractual Plans.   One special problem of sales loads arises in connection with so-called "contractual plans" sold on a "front-end load" basis.   Under these plans, an investor signs up to make monthly investments in a mutual fund over a period of years (although he is not in fact con-

[*218*]

tractually obligated to complete the plan). Under ICA § 27, the sales load on the completed plan may not exceed 9% of the total payments; however, up to 50% of each of the first 12 monthly payments can be deducted for sales compensation. Thus, the typical sales load on a 10-year plan will be 50% of each of the first 12 payments and approximately $4\frac{1}{2}$% of each of the remaining 108 payments.

The problem with this system is that, while it provides a strong incentive to salesmen to get investors started on a plan, it imposes a very heavy sales load on the substantial percentage of investors who stop making payments after a year or two. The SEC, in its 1966 Mutual Fund Report, recommended that Congress prohibit the front-end load and require all fund shares to be sold on a level-load basis. Congress, however, adopted an intermediate approach under which funds may continue to sell shares on a front-end load basis, provided that the fund either (a) does not deduct more than 20% of any payment for sales load, or (b) agrees that the investor may redeem his shares at any time during the first 18 months of the plan and receive (1) the current value of his shares, plus (2) the amount by which the total sales load he has paid exceeds 15% of his total payments into the plan. ICA §§ 27(d), (g).

VII. SANCTIONS FOR VIOLATIONS

The federal securities laws provide for several different types of official sanctions against persons who violate the law, and specify the procedures to be followed in utilizing them.

§ 31. SEC Investigations

The SEC has statutory authority to conduct investigations to determine whether there has been a violation of federal securities law. This authority includes power to subpoena witnesses, administer oaths, and compel the production of books and records anywhere in the United States. SEA § 21; SA §§ 19(b), 20(a). In areas of doubtful jurisdiction, this authority empowers the SEC to conduct an initial inquiry to determine whether the subject of the inquiry is in fact subject to the securities laws. SEC v. Wall St. Transcript Corp., 422 F.2d 1371 (2d Cir. 1970); SEC v. Brigadoon Scotch Distributing Co., 480 F.2d 1047 (2d Cir. 1973).

In general, when information comes to the attention of the Commission indicating that a violation may have occurred, the Commission first conducts an informal inquiry, interviewing witnesses but not serving any compulsory process or taking any sworn statements. If this initial inquiry indicates the existence of a violation, the staff will ask the Commission for a formal order of investigation, which delineates the scope of the investigation and designates the staff members entitled to administer oaths and compel the production of witnesses and records.

The procedures to be followed in "formal investigative proceedings" are set forth in the Commission's Rules Relating to Investigations (RRI), 17 C.F.R. § 203. Under these rules, a witness compelled to testify or produce evidence is entitled to see a copy of the formal order of investigation, RRI 7(a), and to be accompanied, represented and advised by counsel, RRI 7(b), (c). To prevent collusion among witnesses, no witness or his counsel may be present at the examination of any other witness, RRI 7(b); however, the SEC may not bar a witness from being represented by his regular counsel, even though that counsel has also represented other witnesses, unless it can establish that the dual representation will "impede its investigation," SEC v. Csapo, 533 F. 2d 7 (D.C.Cir. 1976). The Commission may for good cause deny a witness the right to obtain a copy of the transcript of his own testimony (although he has an absolute right to inspect the transcript), RRI 6. See Commercial Capital Corp. v. SEC, 360 F.2d 856 (7th Cir. 1966).

The conduct of an SEC investigation is subject to the same testimonial and related privileges as a judicial proceeding, McMann v. SEC, 87 F.2d 377 (2d Cir. 1937), including the attorney-client privilege, the Fourth Amendment prohibition against unreasonable searches and seizures, and the Fifth Amendment privilege against self-incrimination. However, since the securities business is "affected with a public interest" and the securities laws require the maintenance of certain books and records, production of records related to the business may be compelled in spite of Fifth Amendment claims. Shapiro v. U. S., 335 U.S. 1 (1948); SEC v. Olsen, 354 F.2d 166 (2d Cir. 1965).

Although the SEC has statutory authority to publish information concerning violations, SEC § 21(a), its formal investigative proceedings are normally conducted privately, RRI 5, to avoid unwarranted injury to the reputations of the persons being investigated. If the Commission determines to conduct a public investigation in a particular situation, and the record contains implications of wrongdoing by any person, that person must be afforded a reasonable opportunity for cross-examination and for production of rebuttal testimony or documentary evidence. RRI 7(d). However, in a private investigation, a person who knows himself to be a target of the investigation has no right to appear before the staff or the Commission to rebut charges that may have been made against him. See SEC v. National Student Marketing Corp., 538 F.2d 404 (D.C.Cir. 1976).

An SEC investigation may serve as the prelude to several different types of governmental proceedings.

§ 32. SEC Administrative Proceedings

If an SEC investigation uncovers evidence of a violation of the securities laws, the Commission may order an administrative hearing to determine responsibility for the violation and to impose sanctions. An administrative proceeding can only be brought against a person or firm registered with the Commission (such as a broker-dealer, investment adviser, investment company or other regulated entity), or with respect to a security registered with the Commission. Sanctions available in an administrative proceeding include censure, limitations on the registrant's activities, or revocation of registration.

Prior to 1964, the Commission had no direct means of disciplining an employee of a broker-dealer firm who had participated in the firm's illegal activities. However, if such an employee was found to be the "cause" of the suspension or revocation of the firm's registration, he was barred by SEA § 15A(b)(4) from being employed by any other firm which was a member of the NASD. The 1964 Securities Acts Amendments deleted this provision, and gave the Commission direct power to suspend or bar from association with any broker-dealer any person who the Commission finds has violated one or more specified provisions of the 1934 Act. Under the new provision, the SEC began a practice of naming as respondents not only persons associated with the respondent broker-dealer, but also other persons involved in the alleged violation, even though the only possible sanction was to bar them from ever being associated with a broker-dealer. The 1975 amendments put an end to this practice by limiting SEC proceedings to persons "associated, or seeking to become associated, with a broker or dealer." SEA § 15(b)(6).

An administrative hearing is commenced by serving a copy of the Commission's order for the hearing on all named respondents. The hearing is held before an independent Commission employee known as an "administrative law judge" and is generally conducted in the same manner as a non-jury trial, with the Commission staff and the respondents each having the right to present evidence and testimony and to cross-examine witnesses. The hearing may be either public or private in the Commission's discretion (proceedings under the 1933 Act must be public), with respondents often favoring private proceedings to minimize the adverse publicity.

At the conclusion of the hearing, the administrative law judge must file an "initial decision" containing his findings of fact and conclusions of law. This decision may be reviewed by the Commission itself either on petition of one of the parties or on the Commission's own initiative. The Commission is not required to grant a petition for review, but its Rules of Practice provide that it will do so where suspension, denial or revocation of registration is involved. The Commission decides the matter on the basis of briefs and (if requested) oral argument, and may modify the initial decision in any way, including an increase in the sanctions imposed. See Hanly v. SEC, 415 F.2d 589 (2d Cir. 1969).

It is quite common for respondents to make offers of settlement, consenting to lesser sanctions and SEC publication of its findings of violations in exchange for saving the expense and prolonged adverse publicity of a protracted proceeding. The Commission normally insists, as a condition of settlement, that the respondent agree that the Commission may publish its finding as to respondent's violations. Critics of the SEC have charged that the Commission uses its power to force settlements as a means of making and announcing new "law" in essentially non-adversary proceedings.

Under Rule 2(e) of its Rules of Practice, the SEC has asserted its authority to "deny * * * the privilege of appearing or practicing before it to any person who is found by the Commission after notice of and opportunity for hearing," (a) not to possess the requisite qualifications, (b) to be lacking in character or integrity or to have engaged in unethical or improper professional conduct, or (c) to have willfully violated federal securities laws. Under this Rule, the Commission

has disqualified a number of lawyers and accountants from practice before it, despite objections
that any person authorized by state law to practice his profession is entitled to appear before the
SEC. See Emanuel Fields, SA Rel. 5404 (1973).
However, the courts may overturn an SEC disqualification which is not supported by substantial evidence or is procedurally improper. Kivitz
v. SEC, 475 F.2d 956 (D.C.Cir. 1973). Recently a
major accounting firm has challenged the validity
of Rule 2(e), arguing that "the SEC is not authorized by any Act of Congress to conduct disciplinary proceedings or to suspend or disbar accountants or other professionals from practising
before it."   Touche Ross & Co. v. SEC, CCH ¶
95,742 (S.D.N.Y.1976) (complaint).

(a) Judicial Review of SEC Actions

Any party aggrieved by a final order entered
in an SEC administrative proceeding may obtain
review of the order in the United States Court of
Appeals for the District of Columbia or in the
circuit in which the party resides or has its principal place of business. SA § 9; SEA § 25; ICA
§ 43. The courts have on occasion been critical
of the SEC for its failure to enunciate clearly the
legal rules or facts on which it was basing its decisions. See, e. g., Berko v. SEC, 297 F.2d 116
(2d Cir. 1961), 316 F.2d 137 (2d Cir. 1963).
While an administrative agency's determination
will normally be upheld if based on a "preponder-

ance of the evidence," the District of Columbia Court of Appeals has recently held that the SEC can impose certain administrative sanctions only if there is "clear and convincing evidence" of the violation. The court felt that, where the alleged violation involved fraud, and the sanction involved a deprivation of livelihood, the higher standard of proof was more appropriate. Collins Securities Corp. v. SEC, CCH ¶ 96,122 (D.C.Cir. 1977).

The Commission has taken the position that certain of its actions are not "orders" subject to judicial review. These include (a) a decision not to order a company to include a shareholder proposal in its proxy statement, see Medical Committee v. SEC, 432 F.2d 659 (D.C.Cir. 1970), vacated as moot, 404 U.S. 403 (1972), (b) a decision not to object to the action of a stock exchange increasing the minimum commission rates to be charged by its members, see Independent Investor Protective League v. SEC, CCH ¶ 93,270 (2d Cir. 1971) (summary of SEC brief), and (c) the adoption of a rule disqualifying certain types of entities from membership on a stock exchange, see PBW Stock Exchange v. SEC, 485 F.2d 718 (3d Cir. 1973).

With respect to Commission "no-action" positions, the courts have taken the position that if the action involves a routine matter which the Commission properly delegated to its staff and declined to re-examine, there is no "order" subject to judicial review.   Kixmiller v. SEC, 492 F. 2d 641 (D.C.Cir. 1974); see Koss v. SEC, 364 F. Supp. 1321 (S.D.N.Y.1973).   With respect to SEC rule-making proceedings, the 1975 Securities Acts Amendments reversed the holding in the *PBW Stock Exchange* case, *supra,* and authorized persons "adversely affected" by the adoption of an SEC rule to obtain review in a court of appeals. SEA § 25(b).   In addition, courts have held that an SEC rule adoption, while not an "order", is "agency action" subject to judicial review under § 10 of the Administrative Procedure Act.   Independent Broker-Dealer Trade Assn. v. SEC, 442 F.2d 132 (D.C.Cir. 1971);   Natural Resources Defense Council v. SEC, 389 F.Supp. 689 (D.D.C. 1974).

§ 33.   SEC Injunction Actions

In addition to its power to bring administrative proceedings against persons and firms registered with it, the Commission has specific statutory authority to bring an action in a federal district court to enjoin violations of the securities laws by any person.   See, e. g., SEA § 21(d).

Standards for Granting.   In determining whether the SEC has made a "proper showing" for the issuance of an injunction, a court does not apply the "irreparable injury" test applicable to injunction actions by private parties.   The standard generally applied in SEC actions is whether there is a "reasonable likelihood of further violations," although some courts have phrased the test in terms of whether the defendant is shown "to have a propensity or natural inclination to violate the securities laws." Compare SEC v. Manor Nursing Centers, 458 F.2d 1082 (2d Cir. 1972) with SEC v. Bangor Punta Corp., 480 F.2d 341 (2d Cir. 1973). In 1975, the SEC attempted to persuade Congress to amend § 21 of the 1934 Act to permit it to obtain an injunction simply on a showing that the defendant had violated the law, but after protest from the securities bar, Congress rejected the proposed change.

Consequences. In addition to giving rise to a possible contempt citation if the defendant commits another violation of the securities laws, the issuance of an injunction has certain direct consequences. A person who has been enjoined from future violations is disqualified from utilizing the exemption from 1933 Act registration provided by Regulation A, see SA Rule 252(c)(4), (d)(2), or from being associated with a registered investment company, see ICA § 9(a)(2). However, a finding of a violation in an SEC injunctive action has been held not to have collateral estoppel effect in a subsequent private action for damages, on the ground that giving it such effect would constitute a denial of defendant's right to a jury trial on the damage liability question. Rachal v. Hill, 435 F.2d 59 (5th Cir. 1970).

Ancillary Relief. In addition to an injunction against further violations, the SEC will often ask the court for ancillary relief appropriate to the type of violation committed. For example, where the defendant has profited from "insider trading" or manipulative activities, the court may require him to make a rescission offer, see SEC v. Bangor Punta Corp., 331 F.Supp. 1154 (S.D.N.Y. 1971), aff'd with modifications, 480 F.2d 341, 390–91 (2d Cir. 1973), or to turn over his profits to the issuer or to a court-appointed trustee for distribution to persons entitled to them. See SEC v. Texas Gulf Sulphur Co., 446 F.2d 1301 (2d Cir. 1971); SEC v. Golconda Mining Co., 327 F.Supp. 257 (S. D.N.Y.1971). Where the offense involves pervasive corporate mismanagement, the SEC may obtain appointment of a receiver, SEC v. Fifth Avenue Coach Lines, 289 F.Supp. 3 (S.D.N.Y.1968), or of independent directors and special counsel to pursue claims on behalf of the corporation, SEC v. Mattel, Lit.Rels. 6531, 6532 (D.D.C.1974), or of a "special agent" to supervise defendant's compliance with the law, SEC v. Beisinger Industries, 552 F.2d 15 (1st Cir. 1977).

§ 34. Criminal Prosecutions

Willful violations of the securities laws or the rules promulgated under them are punishable by fine and imprisonment. See, e. g., SA § 24; SEA § 32. The Commission does not prosecute criminal cases itself, but transmits the evidence to the

Justice Department, which decides whether to prosecute and handles the prosecution. See SEA § 21(e).

As in criminal prosecutions generally, the "willfulness" requirement means only that the defendant must have intended the act which he did, and does not require a showing that he knew he was violating the securities laws. However, in a criminal prosecution for violation of the antifraud provisions, the government must show more than negligence on defendant's part, even though a showing of negligence might entitle the SEC to an injunction in similar circumstances. U. S. v. Koenig, CCH ¶ 94,765 (S.D.N.Y.1974).

The courts have consistently rejected arguments by defendants that various provisions of the securities laws are unconstitutionally vague when made the basis for criminal prosecutions. See U. S. v. Wolfson, 405 F.2d 779 (2d Cir. 1968).

Conviction of a violation of the securities laws carries with it automatic disqualification from certain benefits or positions, such as the use of the Regulation A exemption, SA Rule 252(c)(3), (d)(1), or association with a registered investment company, ICA § 9(a)(1).

§ 35. SRO Disciplinary Proceedings

In an SEC administrative proceeding against a broker-dealer, one of the sanctions available to the Commission is the suspension or revocation of the respondent's membership in a self-regulatory organization (SRO), such as a national securities exchange or national securities association. In addition, the SRO's themselves are specifically authorized, and indeed required, to impose sanctions on their members for violations of the securities laws or the SROs' own rules. SEA §§ 6(b) (6), 15A(b)(7), 19(g)(1).

In the past, SRO disciplinary proceedings were rather informal, with respondents being accorded few of the protective features associated with governmental sanctions. It has been held, however, that SRO's are sufficiently involved with the SEC to bring their disciplinary actions "within the purview of Fifth Amendment controls over governmental due process." Intercontinental Industries v. American Stock Exchange, 452 F.2d 935 (5th Cir. 1971). Under the 1975 amendments to the Exchange Act, SRO's must notify members of the specific charges against them, give them an opportunity to defend themselves, and support any sanctions with a statement setting forth the specific acts in which the member was found to have engaged, the specific rules which he was found to have violated, and the reasons for the sanction imposed. SEA §§ 6(d)(1), 15A(h)(2).

Prior to 1975, disciplinary actions by the NASD were subject to SEC review, but disciplinary actions by stock exchanges were not. Under the 1975 amendments, reports of all SRO disciplinary actions must be filed with the SEC, and such actions are subject to review by the SEC, either on its own motion or on application of any aggrieved person. If the SEC finds that the respondent engaged in the acts charged, that such acts violated the specified provisions, and that such provisions were applied in a manner consistent with the purposes of the Exchange Act, it is to affirm the sanction; if not, it is to set aside the sanction and, if appropriate, remand the matter to the SRO for further proceedings. The SEC must also set aside the sanction if it is excessive or oppressive or if it imposes any burden on competition not necessary in furtherance of the purposes of the Exchange Act. SEA § 19(e). An SEC order affirming an SRO sanction is subject to court review in the same manner as an SEC sanction imposed in one of its own administrative proceedings.

VIII. CIVIL LIABILITIES

Supplementing the governmental and quasi-governmental sanctions for violations of federal securities law is the possibility of private actions for damages and other relief against alleged violators. The amount of private litigation under federal securities law has grown rapidly in recent years and probably accounts currently for a substantially greater expenditure of effort and expense than does direct government enforcement.

§ 36. Sources of Liability

There are three different types of provisions in the federal securities laws that may give rise to civil liabilities.

The first type is a provision creating an explicit private right of action. The most important of these provisions are SA §§ 11 and 12(2), giving a right of action to purchasers of securities sold by means of misleading statements, SA § 12(1), giving a right of action to purchasers of securities sold in violation of the registration requirements, SEA § 16(b), giving a right of action to an issuer (or a shareholder suing in its behalf) against officers, directors and major shareholders who profit from "short-swing" trading in the issuer's stock, and SEA § 18, giving a right of action to a person who purchases or sells a security in reliance on misleading statements in a report filed under that Act.

The second type is a provision purporting to affect legal relationships between private parties, but not explicitly creating a right of action. Examples of this type are SEA § 29(b) and ICA § 47, which provide that every contract made in violation of the provisions of those respective Acts shall be "void" as regards the rights of specified persons, thus creating an implied private right of action to have the contract declared invalid.

The third type, and by far the most important in terms of the volume of litigation, is the many provisions prohibiting certain actions or declaring them "unlawful." Starting with the famous decision in Kardon v. National Gypsum Co., 69 F. Supp. 512 (E.D.Pa.1946), the courts, applying traditional tort principles, have implied a private right of action on behalf of persons injured by an alleged violation who were within the class of persons that the statutory prohibition was designed to protect. The provisions which have been most extensively used as the basis for private actions of this type are (a) the general anti-fraud prohibitions in SEA §§ 10(b) and 15(c)(1), SA § 17(a), and IAA § 206, and (b) the provisions governing proxy solicitations and tender offers in SEA § 14. While private rights of action have long been recognized under SEA § 10(b), Kardon v. National Gypsum Co., *supra,* courts have recently shown increasing reluctance to extend that recognition to other antifraud provisions. A Second Circuit panel recently decided (2–1) that there was a private right of action under IAA § 206, Abrahamson v. Fleschner, CCH ¶ 95,889 (2d Cir. 1977), but there is considerable doubt as to whether any such right should be recognized under SA § 17(a) because of potential conflict with the express civil liability provisions of that Act. Compare Dorfman v. First Boston Corp., 336 F.Supp. 1089 (E.D.Pa.1972), with Reid

v. Mann, 381 F.Supp. 525 (N.D.Ill.1974). With respect to disclosure requirements, while the courts have recognized a private right of action under the proxy solicitation provisions of SEA § 14 since J. I. Case Co. v. Borak, 377 U.S. 426 (1964), they have recently refused to recognize such a right under the reporting requirements of SEA § 13(a) or the record-keeping requirements of SEA § 17. Lewis v. Elam, CCH ¶ 96,013 (S. D.N.Y.1977); Redington v. Touche Ross, 428 F. Supp. 483 (S.D.N.Y.1977).

The elements of a private right of action under the various substantive provisions of the federal securities laws are described under the appropriate headings in the preceding chapters. The following discussion covers problems relating to all private actions under those laws.

§ 37. Jurisdictional Questions

Under SEA § 27, federal courts have exclusive jurisdiction over actions to enforce any liability under the Exchange Act. Federal and state courts have concurrent jurisdiction of claims under the Securities Act, SA § 22(a), and the Investment Company Act, ICA § 44, although most claims under those laws are also brought in federal courts. Under normal rules of pendent jurisdiction, plaintiffs can, and often do, add counts alleging violation of state common law or statutes to their federal claims under the securities laws.

(a) Venue and Service of Process

The generous venue and service of process provisions of the federal securities laws are an important incentive to plaintiffs to frame their complaints so as to state a claim under those laws. Actions can be brought in any district in which the defendant is found or is an inhabitant or transacts business, and process can be served on any defendant in that district or in any other district in which he can be found. SA § 22; SEA § 27; ICA § 44. However, special venue provisions applicable to certain kinds of defendants may limit the choice available under the securities laws; the Supreme Court has held that a national bank can be sued under the federal securities laws only in a district in which a suit against that bank is permitted by the National Bank Act. Radzanower v. Touche Ross & Co., 426 U.S. 148 (1976).

When a number of private actions involving common questions of fact are brought in different judicial districts, the Judicial Panel on Multidistrict Litigation, pursuant to 28 U.S.C. § 1407, may order consolidated or coordinated pretrial proceedings for all of the pending actions. However, under the 1975 amendments, actions brought by private parties may not be consolidated or coordinated under this provision with an action brought by the Commission, unless the Commission consents. SEA § 21(g).

(b) Statute of Limitations

The specific civil liability provisions of the securities laws contain their own statutes of limitations. An action under SA § 11 or 12(2) must be brought within one year after discovery of the untruth or omission and not more than three years after the sale, while an action under SA § 12(1) must be brought within one year after the violation. SA § 13. An action under SEA § 16(b) must be brought within two years after the insider realized his profit, and an action under SEA § 18 within one year after discovery of the true facts and within three years after the violation. There is no federal statute of limitations applicable to implied rights of action; the courts in those cases look to the law of the state in which the court sits, usually applying either the limitation applicable to actions for fraud or deceit, or the limitation applicable to actions under the state securities law. See IDS Progressive Fund v. First of Michigan Corp., CCH ¶ 95,525 (6th Cir. 1976).

The equitable defense of laches (prejudice to defendant resulting from plaintiff's undue delay in bringing suit) has been held to be available in an action brought under the Exchange Act, even where the action is brought within the time specified in the relevant state statute of limitations and regardless of whether the action is strictly "equitable" in nature. Royal Air Properties v.

Smith, 312 F.2d 210 (9th Cir. 1962). However, the same court has held that defense unavailable in a suit under the specific civil liability provisions of the Securities Act, since those actions are essentially "legal" in nature and since federal law provides a short and definite standard of limitations. Straley v. Universal Uranium and Milling Corp., 289 F.2d 370 (9th Cir. 1961).

§ 38. Plaintiffs

The express civil liability provisions generally specify the persons entitled to sue, although interpretation of these provisions may cause difficulties. Greater difficulties arise in determining who has standing to assert private rights of actions implied from general prohibitions.

In actions based on SEA § 10(b) and Rule 10b–5, the Supreme Court has recently reaffirmed the rule laid down in Birnbaum v. Newport Steel Corp., 193 F.2d 461 (2d Cir. 1952), that suit can only be brought by a person who purchased or sold securities in the transaction in question. See § 21(b) *supra*. It held that even a person to whom securities were offered but not sold has no standing to sue under those provisions. Blue Chip Stamps v. Manor Drug Stores, 421 U.S. 723 (1975). However, in actions attacking mergers and acquisitions under Rule 10b–5, lower courts have interpreted the term "seller" broadly to include any person who is forced to give up securities as a result of the transaction. See, e. g., Drachman v. Harvey, 453 F.2d 722 (2d Cir. 1972).

In actions based on the proxy solicitation and tender offer provisions of SEA § 14, the courts have been generous in granting standing. They have held that violations of the proxy rules may be challenged by the corporation itself, Studebaker Corp. v. Gittlin, 360 F.2d 692 (2d Cir. 1966), or by a shareholder who alleges he was damaged by the deceit practiced on other shareholders to obtain their votes, J. I. Case Co. v. Borak, 377 U. S. 426 (1974). In the case of takeover bids, the courts have held that the target corporation has standing to seek an injunction against violations by the aggressor. Electronic Specialty Co. v. International Controls Corp., 409 F.2d 937 (2d Cir. 1969). However, the Supreme Court has denied standing to a defeated contestant in a takeover bid to seek damages from the target corporation's management and the successful contestant, on the ground that it was not within the class of persons Congress intended to protect by the enactment of SEA § 14(e). Piper v. Chris-Craft Industries, 97 S.Ct. 926 (1977).

In some cases, the courts have rested their decision on standing on broad policy issues, rather than the technical relationship of the plaintiff to the transaction in question. For example, in the Second Circuit decision in the *Piper* case, Judge

Mansfield, concurring, based his recognition of standing "solely on the ground that vigorous enforcement of the antifraud provisions through private litigation calls for [the] implication of a private right of action." See 480 F.2d at 396. However, the Supreme Court decisions in *Blue Chip* and *Piper* seem to reject that rationale as a basis for standing in any situation in which it has not already been recognized. See Stevens, J., dissenting in *Piper,* 97 S.Ct. at 959.

In *Piper,* the Court held that the relevant factors to be examined in determining whether to imply a private right of action under the securities laws were those identified in Cort v. Ash, 422 U.S. 66 (1975): (a) whether the plaintiff is "one of the class for whose especial benefit the statute was enacted," (b) whether there is "any indication of legislative intent, explicit or implicit, either to create such a remedy or to deny one," (c) whether it is "consistent with the underlying purposes of the legislative scheme to imply such a remedy for the plaintiff," and (d) whether "the cause of action [is] one traditionally relegated to state law." 97 Sup.Ct. at 947–49.

(a) Class Actions

Since securities law violations frequently involve a large number of potential claimants, the "class action" provisions of the Federal Rules of Civil Procedure (FRCP) are often utilized to permit one or more of the affected persons to bring an action on behalf of the entire class. As a practical matter, a class action is the only remedy where the damage suffered by each individual plaintiff is too small to warrant the expense of bringing suit.

A class action will only be permitted under FRCP Rule 23 if "(1) the class is so numerous that joinder of all members is impracticable, (2) there are questions of law or fact common to the class, (3) the claims of the representative parties are typical of the claims of the class, and (4) the representative parties will fairly and adequately protect the interests of the class." In addition, the plaintiff must establish either that separate actions would create a risk of inconsistent adjudications, or impairment of the rights of non-parties, or that "the questions of law or fact common to the members of the class predominate over any questions affecting only individual members" and that the class action is "superior to other available methods" for adjudicating the controversy.

In situations involving public offers of securities or publication of allegedly misleading statements that affected the price at which a security was traded in the open market, there is normally no difficulty in establishing that joinder of all parties would be impracticable. See Green v. Wolf Corporation, 406 F.2d 291 (2d Cir. 1968); Cannon v. Texas Gulf Sulphur Co., 47 F.R.D. 60

(S.D.N.Y.1969). With respect to plaintiff's status as an adequate representative of the class, it is normally not difficult to find a plaintiff who has a "typical" claim and no conflicting interests. A question may be raised as to the competence of the plaintiff's attorney, who is often the moving force in bringing a class action, to represent the interests of the class, but the courts have not been overly sympathetic to defendants' expressions of concern on this question. See Dolgow v. Anderson, 43 F.R.D. 472 (E.D.N.Y.1968).

There is often a more difficult question as to whether the common issues of law or fact predominate over the separate issues. Where the gravamen of the complaint is oral misrepresentations, the court will be reluctant to permit a class action. Moscarelli v. Stamm, 288 F.Supp. 453 (E.D.N.Y.1968). Where misstatements of a similar nature are made in a series of prospectuses or other documents, the court may divide the class of plaintiffs into subclasses pursuant to FRCP Rule 23(c)(4)(B). See Green v. Wolf Corp., *supra*.

(b) Derivative Actions

In cases involving mergers or acquisitions or alleged management misconduct, the action is often brought by a shareholder suing derivatively on behalf of the corporation. In merger cases, the action may be framed in terms of both individual and derivative claims, with the courts not always being too precise about which form is appropriate. See J. I. Case Co. v. Borak, 377 U.S. 426 (1964).

Any derivative action brought in a federal court must comply with FRCP Rule 23.1. That rule requires, *inter alia,* that the plaintiff have been a shareholder at the time of the transaction complained of and that he "allege with particularity" the efforts he has made to secure the desired action from the directors and, "if necessary," the shareholders. Although the requirement of prior demand on the directors is normally waived where the board is under the domination of the defendants in the action, recent decisions in derivative actions brought under the Investment Company Act have interpreted that requirement very strictly where a majority of the board was "independent" of the alleged wrongdoers. In Kauffman Mutual Fund Actions, 479 F.2d 257 (1st Cir. 1973), the court held that general allegations of "domination and control" of the board by the defendants were insufficient to excuse demand, and in Lasker v. Burks, 404 F. Supp. 1172 (S.D.N.Y.1975), the court held that, where the "disinterested" directors, acting as a group, had decided in good faith that the corporation should not sue, plaintiff was barred from pursuing a derivative action on its behalf.

With respect to the rather cryptic requirement in FRCP 23.1 that plaintiff make prior demand on the shareholders "if necessary," one federal court has held that even though prior demand on shareholders would be required in a state court action in that jurisdiction, it would not be required in an action under the Investment Company Act where its effect would be to "negate the intendment" of that Act to protect investors. Levitt v. Johnson, 334 F.2d 815 (1st Cir. 1965).

Actions under SEA § 16(b) to recover "short-swing" profits on behalf of a corporation are governed by the specific provisions of that section, which require prior demand on the directors. However, the courts have consistently held, contrary to the normal rule governing derivative actions, that the plaintiff in a § 16(b) action need not have been a shareholder at the time of the transactions involved, either because such a requirement would be inconsistent with the purposes of that section, Blau v. Mission Corp., 212 F.2d 77 (2d Cir. 1954), or because the statute creates a new primary right of action which is not a derivative action in the traditional sense, Dottenheim v. Murchison, 227 F.2d 737 (5th Cir. 1955).

(c) Bars to Recovery

The general rules of law barring suit by a plaintiff who has waived his rights or otherwise estopped himself from making a claim, or who is found to be *in pari delicto* with the defendant, are applicable in securities cases, but with important limitations.

Waiver and Estoppel. Both the 1933 Act and the 1934 Act provide that "any condition, stipulation, or provision binding any person to waive compliance with any provision of [the Act] shall be void," SA § 14; SEA § 29(a). Notwithstanding those provisions, the Ninth Circuit has held that the common law defenses of waiver and estoppel are available in suits under either Act. Straley v. Universal Uranium and Milling Corp., 289 F.2d 370 (1961); Royal Air Properties v. Smith, 312 F.2d 210 (1962). The Fifth Circuit, on the other hand, held that under SA § 14, plaintiff could not be held to have waived his rights by refusing defendant's offer to repurchase illegally sold securities, but that he could be estopped if defendant had made an unconditional tender and demand for return of the securities. Meyers v. C & M Petroleum Producers, 476 F.2d 427 (1973).

In Wilko v. Swan, 346 U.S. 427 (1953), the Supreme Court held that a customer's agreement with his broker to arbitrate any dispute with respect to his account could not be raised as a defense to an action by the customer under SA § 12(2) for alleged misrepresentations in the sale of stock. The Court said that the agreement to arbitrate was a "stipulation" to waive compliance with the Act, within the meaning of § 14, and was therefore void. In Scherk v. Alberto Culver Co., 417 U.S. 506 (1974), however, the Court held (5–4) that an agreement to arbitrate would be given effect to bar an implied right of action under SEA § 10(b), where the agreement involved an international transaction between a large American corporation and a foreign national.

Pari Delicto. Courts have traditionally denied relief to plaintiffs who are found to be *in pari delicto* with defendants or, in cases seeking equitable relief, if the plaintiff does not come into court with "clean hands." In actions under the securities laws, plaintiffs are generally not barred from suit because they participated in the illegal activities, at least where their culpability is less than that of defendants. Can-Am Petroleum Co. v. Beck, 331 F.2d 371 (10th Cir. 1964). Two appellate courts have held, however, that a "tippee" is barred by the "clean hands" doctrine from suing his "tipper", when he bought stock on the basis of "inside information" that turned out to be false. Tarasi v. Pittsburgh Nat'l Bank, 555 F.2d 1152 (3d Cir. 1977); Kuehnert v. Texstar Corp., 412 F.2d 700 (5th Cir. 1969). But one court has held that a tipper should be able to sue in these circumstances since he is generally less culpable than the tipper. Nathanson v. Weis, Voisin & Cannon, 325 F.Supp. 50 (S.D.N.Y.

1971). The argument for permitting plaintiffs to sue in these cases is the "prophylactic effect" of private damage actions in discouraging violations of the securities laws. Following this line of reasoning, one court has permitted a customer to sue his broker for losses resulting from an illegal extension of credit, even though the customer knowingly instituted the illegal transaction while the broker merely acted to accommodate him. Pearlstein v. Scudder & German, 429 F.2d 1136 (2d Cir. 1970), modified 527 F.2d 114 (2d Cir. 1975); but see Gordon v. duPont Glore Forgan, 487 F.2d 1260 (5th Cir. 1973).

Contributory Negligence. The provisions creating explicit private rights of action for misleading statements bar the plaintiff from recovery only if he *knew* of the untruth or omission. SA §§ 11(a), 12(2); SEA § 18(a). With respect to implied private rights of action under the antifraud provisions, courts have generally held that plaintiff must establish that he himself exercised "due diligence" to be entitled to recover. However, in light of the Supreme Court's decision in Ernst & Ernst v. Hochfelder, § 39(b) *infra,* that *scienter* on the part of the *defendant* must be shown to maintain an action under the antifraud provisions, recent decisions have held that a plaintiff is not barred by ordinary negligence, but only if he "intentionally refused to investigate, 'in disregard of a risk known to him or so obvious that he must be taken to have been aware of it, and so great as to make it highly probable that harm would follow.' " Dupuy v. Dupuy, 551 F.2d 1005 (5th Cir. 1977).

§ 39. Defendants

The primary perpetrators of securities violations are often persons or entities from whom it is impossible to obtain any financial recovery. Plaintiffs will therefore attempt to include as defendants more solvent individuals or entities who have had some connection with the violation— "deep pockets" from which a judgment can be paid. Among the types of parties often named as secondary defendants are the employer of an individual wrongdoer; directors of a corporate wrongdoer; underwriters, broker-dealers, banks or agents that participated in the transaction; accountants; lawyers; and self-regulatory organizations.

In actions under SA § 11, the liability of persons having specified relationships to the issuer is spelled out in considerable detail. In actions under other sections, however, the liabilities of secondary defendants must be determined under such doctrines as agency liability, aiding and abetting, conspiracy, tort liability, and contribution and indemnification.

(a) Liability of Principal

These are two independent bases for holding a brokerage firm or other principal liable for securities violations by its employees or agents. Under traditional agency rules, a principal is liable for damages caused to a third party by an agent who had authority, apparent authority, or "agency power" to make representations on the principal's behalf. Rest. (2d), Agency § 257. In addition, SA § 15 and SEA § 20 make any person who "controls" another person jointly and severally liable to any third party to whom the controlled person incurs liability under those Acts. However, the controlling person can escape liability if he can show that "he acted in good faith and did not induce the act constituting the violation" (SEA § 20) or "had no knowledge or reasonable ground to believe in the existence of the facts" giving rise to the violation (SA § 15).

The principal question that has arisen in reconciling these sources of liability is whether, if the defendant establishes the "good faith" or "lack of knowledge" defense available under the statute, it relieves him of his liability under traditional agency principles as well as his statutory liability as a "controlling person." Some courts have held that establishment of the statutory defense does not bar recovery on agency grounds, since Congress' purpose in the "controlling person" provisions was to extend liability to new classes of persons and not to restrict the application of existing bases of recovery. Holloway v. Howerdd, 536 F. 2d 690 (6th Cir. 1976); Fey v. Walston & Co., 493 F.2d 1036 (7th Cir. 1974). Others have held, however, that the "controlling person" provisions are the only basis for holding a principal liable for his agent's violations of the securities laws. Rochez Bros. v. Rhoades, 527 F.2d 880 (3rd Cir. 1975). One court has taken the intermediate position that *some* agency principles may be applicable, at least in SEC enforcement proceedings. SEC v. Management Dynamics, 515 F.2d 801 (2d Cir. 1975).

(b) Aiding and Abetting

The idea that an "aider and abettor" is jointly liable with the actual perpetrator of an offense has its roots both in the criminal law and in § 876 of the Restatement of Torts, which imposes liability on a person who knowingly "gives substantial assistance and encouragement" to another person's breach of duty. One court, in a securities fraud case, held that "three elements are required for liability: (1) that an independent wrong exist; (2) that the aider or abettor knew of the wrong's existence; and (3) that substantial assistance be given in effecting that wrong." Landy v. FDIC, 486 F.2d 139, 162 (3d Cir. 1973). In addition to asserting liability against someone as an "aider and abettor", plaintiff may also seek to hold him liable as a party to a conspiracy to violate the securities laws. While establishment of a "conspiracy" in a criminal prosecution involves quite different elements than a case of "aiding and abetting", the opinions in the securities cases in which a conspiracy count has been added have not generally taken pains to distinguish the two theories. See, e. g., H. L. Green Co. v. Childree, 185 F.Supp. 95 (S.D.N.Y.1960); SEC v. National Bankers Life Ins. Co., 324 F. Supp. 189 (N.D.Tex.), aff'd, 448 F.2d 652 (5th Cir. 1971). The following discussion is therefore cast in terms of the elements of aiding and abetting, rather than those of conspiracy.

With respect to the knowledge requirement, the most important question is whether a defendant can be held liable for aiding and abetting a violation where he did not have actual knowledge but would have discovered the violation if he had exercised reasonable care. The answer to this question may depend on (i) the section of the securities laws cited as the basis for liability, (ii) the relationship of the named defendant to the principal wrongdoer, and (iii) the circuit in which the action is brought.

The Supreme Court recently held that an accounting firm could not be held liable for aiding and abetting a securities fraud under SEA Rule 10b–5 merely on the basis of its alleged negligence in failing to discover the fraud. Ernst &

Ernst v. Hochfelder, 425 U.S. 185 (1976). The court rested its decision on a general holding that no action would lie against any defendant under Rule 10b–5 without an allegation of scienter, or intent to defraud, and disclaimed any intention to define the elements necessary to constitute "aiding and abetting." 425 U.S. at 191 n. 7. Nevertheless, its decision would indicate that no defendant could be held liable as an aider and abettor under the *anti-fraud* provisions unless he had actual knowledge of the fraud or unless his willful disregard of the facts available to him was equivalent to *scienter*.

In an SEC injunction action charging an attorney with aiding and abetting a violation of SA § 5 by *negligently* giving an opinion that certain securities could be sold without registration, the Second Circuit held that "the negligence standard [is] sufficient in the context of enforcement proceedings seeking equitable or prophylactic relief." SEC v. Spectrum Ltd., 489 F.2d 535 (1973). However, both the Second Circuit and the Supreme Court have frequently held different standards applicable in SEC enforcement actions and private actions for damages. See Ernst & Ernst v. Hochfelder, 425 U.S. at 194 n. 12; SEC v. Texas Gulf Sulphur Co., 401 F.2d 833 (2d Cir. 1968).

The degree of knowledge required to hold a director liable for securities law violations by his company is a matter of some uncertainty. In

Lanza v. Drexel & Co., 479 F.2d 1277 (2d Cir. 1973), plaintiffs had purchased securities from a company on the basis of misleading statements made to them by the company's officers. In a suit under SEA Rule 10b–5, they attempted to assert liability against an "outside" director of the company (and the brokerage firm of which he was a partner), on the alternative grounds that (i) defendant had an affirmative duty, as a director, to assure that all material adverse information was conveyed to purchasers of the company's securities, and (ii) sufficient "disquieting facts" had come to his attention about the company's financial condition that he should have made further inquiries before voting to approve the transaction. In an *en banc* decision (6–4), the court held that (i) a director has no independent "duty to convey" information, and (ii) defendant's failure to make further inquiry amounted at most to negligence, and that he could not be held liable as an aider and abettor, a conspirator, or a participant in a Rule 10b–5 violation unless "willful or reckless disregard for the truth" were shown.

The four dissenting judges argued for a "flexible" standard under which the degree of *scienter* required to establish liability would vary with the relationship of the particular defendant to the other parties to the transaction. The Ninth Circuit subsequently adopted a similar "flexible standard" approach. White v. Abrams, 495 F.2d 724

(1974). However, the Supreme Court's decision in Ernst & Ernst v. Hochfelder, *supra,* appears to resolve the issue in favor of the approach taken by the majority in *Lanza.*

The situation is different, however, with respect to directors' liability for a company's violation of SEA § 14 and Rule 14a–9 by dissemination of a misleading proxy statement. In Gould v. American-Hawaiian Steamship Co., 535 F.2d 761 (3d Cir. 1976), the court held that a director could be held liable in damages for negligence in failing to make a careful review of the proxy materials. However, the court did not rely on an aiding and abetting or conspiracy theory, holding simply that a director has implied liability under SEA § 14 for a misleading proxy statement analogus to his explicit liability under SA § 11 for a misleading registration statement. (Since most merger proxy statements are now also 1933 Act registration statements under SA Rule 145 (see § 10(d) *supra*), this decision produces a consistency of result in merger cases.)

With respect to the requirement that the aider and abettor give "substantial assistance" in effecting the wrong, the recurrent question has been whether someone can be held liable for *failing* to take action to prevent the violation. In Brennan v. Midwestern United Life Ins. Co., 286 F.Supp. 702 (N.D.Ind.1968), aff'd, 417 F.2d 147 (7th Cir. 1969), the district court held that an issuer could be held liable for failure to report fraudulent activities in its own stock of which it was aware. The Court of Appeals, in affirming the decision, held that "Midwestern's acquiescence through silence * * * combined with its affirmative acts was a form of aiding and abetting," but declined to decide "whether the failure to report [the] activities * * * would in itself give rise to liability under Rule 10b–5." However, at least one court has held an issuer and one of its principal officers liable in damages for failing to correct a broker-dealer's misrepresentations of the issuer's prospective earnings. Green v. Jonhop, 358 F.Supp. 413 (D.Or.1973).

The persons most concerned about liability for failure to act are accountants and lawyers, who may in the course of their activities learn of securities law violations by their clients or others. The issues are complicated by the fact that liability may be asserted against them either on the ground that they aided and abetted (or participated in) the violation, or that they had an independent duty to disclose their knowledge to the victims or intended victims of the violations.

In Wessel v. Buhler, 437 F.2d 279 (9th Cir. 1971), the court held that an accounting firm could not be held liable under Rule 10b–5 for failure to disclose to prospective investors its knowledge of irregularities and deficiencies in its client's financial statements. A similar approach was followed in Fischer v. Kletz, 266 F.Supp. 180 (S.D.N.Y.1967), at least as to unaudited interim financial statements. However, the court in *Fischer* indicated that accountants could be held liable for common law deceit, and perhaps also under Rule 10b–5, for failing to disclose information showing that financial statements which they had previously certified were inaccurate and misleading.

The SEC has taken the position that an attorney who learns that his client is engaged in a transaction which violates the securities laws has an obligation to refuse to give an opinion as to the validity of the transaction, to insist that the client comply with the securities laws, and, if the client refuses, to inform the SEC of the violation. The validity of this position has not yet been adjudicated by the courts, see SEC v. National Student Marketing Corp., CCH ¶ 93,820 (D.D.C. 1973) (preliminary motions), CCH ¶ 96,027 (D. D.C.1977) (approval of settlement), nor has the related question of an attorney's possible liability in damages to persons injured in such a transaction.

One court has held, in a suit for sale of unregistered securities, that an attorney who "was present at every turn" in the transaction, had reason to know that registration was required, and "might have prevented the sale", was nevertheless not liable as "a party to the sale" under

SA § 12(1). Nicewarner v. Blevins, 244 F.Supp. 261 (D.Colo.1965). However, two cases arising under the Oregon Blue Sky law have taken a broader view of an attorney's liability, holding that an attorney who prepares the legal papers required to complete a sale of securities which violates that law is liable to purchasers as a "participant" in the transaction. Adams v. American Western Securities, 510 P.2d 838 (Or.1973); Black & Co. v. Nova-Tech, 333 F.Supp. 468 (D. Or.1971).

(c) Indemnification and Contribution

After recovery of a judgment against one or more defendants in a private damage action, a particular defendant may claim (a) indemnification by another party against his entire liability, or (b) contribution by other parties toward satisfaction of the judgment.

There is no specific provision governing indemnification in the federal securities laws; the SEC's position with respect to indemnification of directors, officers and underwriters in public offerings registered under the 1933 Act is discussed in § 8 *supra*. In an action under SEA Rule 10b–5, a defendant who was found guilty of fraud was held not to be entitled to indemnification from another wrongdoer, but a company which was only vicariously liable for the wrongdoing of its agent was held to be entitled to indemnification.

deHaas v. Empire Petroleum Co., 286 F.Supp. 809 (D.Colo.1969), aff'd in part, 435 F.2d 1223 (10th Cir. 1970).

On the other hand, in an action under § 14(a), corporate directors who were held liable for negligence in connection with a misleading proxy statement were denied indemnification on policy grounds similar to those enunciated by the SEC with respect to 1933 Act registration statements. Gould v. American-Hawaiian Steamship Co., 387 F.Supp. 163 (D.Del.1974), aff'd, 535 F.2d 761 (3d Cir. 1976).

In contrast to the situation regarding indemnification, several of the civil liability provisions of the securities laws contain specific language permitting any person held liable under those provisions to obtain contribution, "as in cases of contract," from any other person who, if joined as a defendant, would have been required to make the same payment. SA § 11(f); SEA §§ 9(e), 18(b). See Globus v. Law Research Service, 318 F.Supp. 955 (S.D.N.Y.1970), aff'd, 442 F.2d 1346 (2d Cir. 1971). On the basis of these provisions, an implied right to contribution has also been recognized in actions under SEA Rule 10b–5. deHaas v. Empire Petroleum Co., *supra*. Since contribution is to be "as in cases of contract" it will generally involve allocation of damages pro rata rather than in accordance with degree of fault. See Globus v. Law Research Service, *su-*

pra. However, SA § 11(f) bars recovery of contribution by any person guilty of fraudulent misrepresentation from a person not guilty thereof, and a similar approach might well be followed under other sections.

§ 40. Damages

The remedy most commonly sought in a private action under the federal securities laws is damages for the financial loss allegedly caused by defendant's wrongdoing. Because of the great variety of situations giving rise to liability, it is difficult to generalize about the computation of damages. There are, however, certain types of transactions which lend themselves to particular theories of liability, and certain common questions which can arise in any type of securities case because of the distinctive attributes of securities and the entities which issue them.

Direct Damages. The simplest situation is where the plaintiff is suing the other party to a transaction in which he bought or sold securities. If plaintiff is a buyer, alleging that he bought securities sold under a misleading registration statement, the measure of recovery under SA § 11(e) is the difference between the price he paid for the security and either its value at the time he brought suit or the price at which he disposed of it. However, the seller may reduce or defeat the recovery to the extent that he can show that the decline in value resulted from something other than the misstatements in the registration statement. See Beecher v. Able, § 11(a) *supra*. If the suit is for sale of unregistered securities or for misrepresentation under SA § 12, the buyer may sue either for a full refund of the purchase price, on tender of the security, or for "damages" (normally the difference between his purchase price and the price at which he disposed of it) if he no longer owns it.

If the plaintiff is a seller, alleging that the buyer misrepresented or withheld material facts, his suit will generally be to enforce the implied civil liability under SEA § 10(b) and Rule 10b–5. In this situation, the courts have generally held that the measure of damages is the difference between the price he received and "the fair value of what he would have received had there been no fraudulent conduct." Affiliated Ute Citizens v. U. S., 406 U.S. 128, 155 (1972). However, if the security has increased in value since the transaction, the court will often award the plaintiff the difference between the sale price and the current value (or the price realized by the defendant on resale), on the ground that the "windfall" should more properly go to the wronged party than the wrongdoer. See Janigan v. Taylor, 344 F.2d 781 (1st Cir. 1965). A second rationale supporting this result is that if the defendant had not induced the transaction by his misrepresentations, the plaintiff would have realized the profit himself. Zeller v. Bogue, 476 F.2d 795, 802 n. 10 (2d Cir. 1973). However, the courts have not extended this approach to the situation where a merger is approved on the basis of a misleading proxy statement and the properties of the acquired company increase in value following the merger. Gerstle v. Gamble-Skogmo, 478 F.2d 1281 (2d Cir. 1973).

Indirect Damages. Where the plaintiff is suing someone other than the opposite party in a transaction, the basic rule of damages is hard to formulate. Plaintiffs in these cases (they are normally class or derivative actions) may have bought or sold securities in stock exchange transactions, and are suing the issuer for having affected the market price by misleading statements, or are suing people who were trading on "inside" information at about the same time. Or former shareholders in a merged company may sue the surviving company, alleging that the merger was procured, or the merger ratio affected, by a misleading proxy statement. The problem is that any "loss" suffered by the plaintiffs is matched by a "profit" realized not by the defendant but by other innocent parties, and the aggregate of all plaintiffs' "losses" may far exceed any "profit" realized by the wrongdoing defendants. See Fridrich v. Bradford, § 19(b) *supra*. In these situations, the courts have tended to duck the damage question, see Shapiro v. Merrill Lynch, § 19(b) *supra,* in the hope that defendants will come up with a settlement offer which will be sufficient to pay the fees of the attorneys for the plaintiff class, with some significant amount left over for distribution to those members of the plaintiff class who can be located and induced to file claims. See, e. g., Cannon v. Texas Gulf Sulphur Co., CCH ¶ 93,432 (S.D.N.Y.1972).

Common Problems. In cases where damages are to be determined on the basis of the difference between the "price" paid or received in a transaction and the "value" of the security at a particular time, a number of problems may arise.

Price. Where the transaction is for cash, the price must be adjusted to reflect other payments in connection with the transaction. When it is an exchange of one security for another, the "price" paid or received for one is the "value" of the other, and the valuation of the consideration can produce very large changes in the measure of damages. See Allis-Chalmers Mfg. Co. v. Gulf & Western Industries, 372 F.Supp. 570 (N.D.Ill. 1974), rev'd on other grounds, 527 F.2d 335 (7th Cir. 1975).

Value. Determination of the "value" that a security would have had at a particular time if all relevant facts had been known is not an easy matter. In some cases, the court looks to the price which the security reached after the facts became known and the market had had a reasonable period to absorb the new information. See, e. g., Mitchell v. Texas Gulf Sulphur Co., 446 F.2d 90 (10th Cir. 1971). However, the market price may have been affected in the meantime by factors other than disclosure of those particular facts. See SA § 11(e). Even the market price on a date when all relevant facts were public may not be considered the "value" on that date if it can be shown that the market was affected by "panic selling" or other unusual influences. Beecher v. Able, § 11(a) *supra*.

Large Blocks. The per share "value" of a large block of stock is not necessarily the same as the current market price of that stock in small transactions. When the block represents a controlling interest in the company, it may be valued at a premium over the current market price. Newmark v. RKO General, 425 F.2d 348 (2d Cir. 1970). But when it represents a minority interest in a company of which someone else has control, it may be valued at a substantial discount from the current market. Chris-Craft Industries v. Piper Aircraft Corp., 516 F.2d 172 (2d Cir. 1975), rev'd on other grounds, 97 S.Ct. 926 (1977).

Consequential Damages. When the violation consists of an improper course of conduct by a broker-dealer or other professional, there will often be a question of how much of the customer's trading losses can be charged to the defendant. If a court finds that the customer would not have entered into the transactions except for the defendant's violation, it is likely to charge the defendant with all of the customer's losses on those transactions. Chasins v. Smith Barney, 438 F.2d 1167 (2d Cir. 1970) (nondisclosure of market-maker status); Landry v. Hemphill Noyes, 473 F.2d 365 (1st Cir. 1973) (margin violation). On the other hand, where the violation consists of improper handling of the customer's account, the court may limit the recovery to the damages directly resulting from the violation. Hecht v. Harris Upham, 283 F.Supp. 417 (N.D.Cal.1968), aff'd with modifications, 430 F.2d 1202 (9th Cir. 1970).

Punitive Damages. One of the principal reasons for allowing private rights of action, particularly where there is no plaintiff who suffers any ascertainable "damage" (e. g., insider trading in a public market), is to discourage violations by depriving the violator of his illegal profits. It would therefore seem logical, at least in that type of case, to permit recovery of punitive damages as an additional deterrent. However, the courts have held that punitive damages are barred by SEA § 28(a), which provides that "no person * * * shall recover * * * a total amount in excess of his actual damages" in a suit under that Act, even though the language of that sec-

tion is clearly aimed at preventing a double recovery under state and federal law, rather than
at punitive damages. Green v. Wolf Corp., 406
F.2d 291 (2d Cir. 1968). Punitive damages have
also been held to be unavailable in an action under the antifraud provisions of SA § 17(a), on
the ground that the additional deterrent effect
they might provide is outweighed by other policy
considerations. Globus v. Law Research Service,
418 F.2d 1276 (2d Cir. 1969). However, if plaintiff combines his federal securities law claims
with a common law fraud claim, he may be able
to recover punitive damages on the latter claim
in the same action. Coffee v. Permian Corp., 474
F.2d 1040 (5th Cir. 1973).

§ 41. Equitable Relief

The federal securities laws contemplate "suits
in equity" as well as "actions at law" by aggrieved persons. SA § 22(a); SEA § 27. As an
alternative to damages, private plaintiffs may
seek rescission of a transaction, an injunction
against threatened or further violations, or other
forms of equitable relief.

Rescission. The Securities Act specifically con-
templates rescission as the appropriate remedy
where defendant has sold securities without registration, or by means of misleading statements,
and plaintiff still retains the securities. SA § 12.
In actions under the Securities Exchange Act,

plaintiffs may seek rescission pursuant to SEA § 29(b), which provides that all contracts made in violation of the Act shall be void as against the violators. However, in the kinds of actions that are generally brought under that Act, rescission is often an impracticable or inappropriate remedy.

For example, where plaintiff is an aggrieved seller who claims defendant purchased securities from him without disclosing material facts, rescission may be unavailable because of an intervening restructuring of the issuing company, or the resale of the securities to a third party. And where a merger has been approved and consummated on the basis of a misleading proxy solicitation in violation of SEA § 14, the courts have held that SEA § 29(b) does not require that the merger be set aside, and that plaintiff will normally be limited to money damages because of the practical difficulties and hardship to public shareholders that equitable relief would entail. Mills v. Electric Auto-Lite Co., 396 U.S. 375 (1970), and on remand, CCH ¶ 93,354 (N.D.Ill. 1972). On the other hand, one court has ordered a new election of directors when the original election was tainted by a misleading proxy statement. Gladwin v. Medfield Corp., 540 F.2d 1266 (5th Cir. 1976).

Injunctions. The situations most appropriate for injunctive relief under the securities laws are mergers and tender offers, which are both subject to disclosure requirements under SEA § 14. Persons who believe that the disclosures are inadequate can seek a preliminary injunction against the holding of a shareholder's meeting or the acceptance of tendered shares until adequate disclosures have been made. See Studebaker Corp. v. Gittlin, 360 F.2d 692 (2d Cir. 1966); General Host Corp. v. Triumph American, 359 F.Supp. 749 (S.D.N.Y.1973). The courts have taken the view that they should be generous in granting preliminary temporary relief prior to consummation of the transaction, because "the opportunity for doing equity * * * is considerably better than it will be later on." Electronic Specialty Co. v. International Controls Corp., 409 F.2d 937 (2d Cir. 1969).

Private plaintiffs have sometimes taken a position, similar to that of the SEC, that they should be entitled to an injunction against further violations by any person who is shown to have committed a securities law violation. However, in Rondeau v. Mosinee Paper Corp., 422 U.S. 49 (1975), the Supreme Court rejected this position and held that applications for injunctions by private plaintiffs under the federal securities laws should be judged by traditional equitable standards, requiring the plaintiff to show danger of irreparable harm and other usual prerequisites for injunctive relief.

Other Forms of Relief. In private actions, as in SEC actions, involving looting or a pervasive pattern of violations, the court may order appointment of a receiver or other structural changes to prevent a repetition of the illegal activity. For example, in a recent action by shareholders against the directors of a major oil company for violating SEC proxy rules by failing to disclose illegal payments and political contributions, the court approved a settlement providing for a majority of "independent outside directors" on the board, the appointment of an audit committee, the nomination of six named persons as directors, and other relief. Gilbar v. Keeler, Civ. No. 75–611–EAC (C.D.Cal.1976).

IX. EXTRATERRITORIAL APPLICATION

The increasing "internationalization" of securities markets in recent years has raised difficult questions as to when, and to what extent, U. S. securities laws will apply to transactions which have connections with the U. S. and with one or more other countries. The transactions fall into three categories: (1) U. S. transactions in foreign securities; (2) foreign transactions in U. S. securities; and (3) foreign transactions in foreign securities which have some impact on U. S. investors or markets. Within each of these categories, several different questions can arise: (1) whether a U. S. court or the SEC has subject matter jurisdiction over the transaction involved; (2) whether the court can obtain personal jurisdiction over foreign defendants; (3) whether it is appropriate for U. S. courts to exercise jurisdiction under applicable principles of international law; and (4) whether a U. S. court or the SEC can fashion and enforce effective relief.

Many of the substantive provisions of the securities laws speak in terms of "the use of facilities of interstate commerce or of the mails" to effect a specified transaction. The term "interstate commerce" is defined in SA § 2(7) and SEA § 3(a)(17) to include commerce between any foreign country and the U. S., so that international transactions of that type are clearly covered. Under SEA § 30(b), that Act does "not apply to any person insofar as he transacts a business in securities without the jurisdiction of the United States," but the meaning of "jurisdiction" in that context is unclear.

In an action under either the 1933 Act or the 1934 Act, process may be served on any defendant, "wherever the defendant may be found." SA § 22(a); SEA § 27. The courts have held, however, that to satisfy due process requirements, "the person sought to be charged must know, or have good reason to know, that his conduct will have effect in the state seeking to assert jurisdiction over him." Leasco v. Maxwell, 468 F.2d 1326 (2d Cir. 1972).

§ 42. U. S. Transactions in Foreign Securities

Public Offerings to U. S. Investors. Public offerings to U. S. investors by foreign issuers are of course subject to the registration requirements of the 1933 Act to the same extent as offerings by domestic issuers. Indeed, Schedule B to the Act sets forth special disclosure requirements for the registration of securities issued by foreign governments (which do not share in the exemption for U. S. Federal, state and local government securities).

Foreign issuers are also entitled to the same exemptions as domestic issuers (except for Regulation A, which under SA Rule 252(a)(1) is available only to U. S. and Canadian issuers). However, the entire offering must meet the terms of the exemption; a foreign issuer cannot claim the "private offering" exemption under SA § 4(2) for a single sale to a U. S. purchaser in conjunction with a general public offering in another country.

U. S. Trading in Foreign Securities. More difficult problems arise with respect to securities of foreign issuers which are purchased by U. S. investors in secondary transactions and come to be traded on U. S. exchanges or in the over-the-counter markets. Under SEA §§ 12, 13, 14 and

16, issuers of all exchange-listed and certain OTC securities must register with the SEC and file annual and current reports, and are subject to rules governing proxy solicitations and insider trading (see § 12 *supra*). Since the foreign issuers in most of these situations have made no securities offerings in the U. S. and are not subject to U. S. jurisdiction in any way, there is no way for the SEC to enforce these requirements, other than to suspend U. S. trading in the securities, which would do much more harm to the U. S. investors than to the foreign issuers.

When the Securities Exchange Act was amended in 1964 to extend its coverage to OTC securities, these practical considerations led to suggestions that foreign issuers be exempted from the Act's requirements, Congress, however, was unwilling to appear to treat foreign issuers more leniently than domestic issuers, and instead gave the SEC authority to exempt foreign issuers if it found such exemptions to be "in the public interest and consistent with the protection of investors." SEA § 12(g)(3). After much deliberation and delicate international negotiations, the SEC adopted SEA Rule 12g3–2, under which the securities of a foreign issuer are exempt from § 12(g) if the issuer, or the government of its home country, furnishes the SEC each year with copies of all information material to investors which it has made public in its home country during the preceeding year. A list identifying the items of information must also be furnished to the SEC, but there is no requirement that either the list or the information be translated into English.

§ 43. Foreign Transactions in U. S. Securities

Foreign Public Offerings by U. S. Issuers. A foreign investor who purchases securities in an offering registered under the 1933 Act has the same right of action as a U. S. purchaser in the event there is a material misstatement or omission in the registration statement. However, the SEC has taken the position that, since the principal purpose of the 1933 Act is to protect U. S. investors, it will not make any objection to a U. S. corporation making a public offering of its securities abroad, solely to foreign investors, without registration under the Act, provided that the offering is made under circumstances reasonably designed to preclude redistribution of the securities within the U. S. or to American investors. SA Rel. 4708 (1964). The SEC has not taken a position on how long the securities must remain in foreign hands before they will be deemed to have "come to rest" and be free to be resold to U. S. investors. Large amounts of "Eurodollar" bonds have been publicly offered and sold by subsidiaries of U. S. corporations to foreign investors pursuant to this SEC interpretation.

Even if a foreign offering by a U. S. issuer is exempt from the 1933 Act registration requirements, a foreign purchaser may still be able to state a claim under the antifraud provision of the federal securities laws if misrepresentations were made in connection with the transaction. See Wandschneider v. Industrial Incomes, CCH ¶ 93,433 (S.D.N.Y.1972).

In contrast to its position on foreign offerings by U. S. industrial companies, the SEC has held that a U. S. mutual fund offering its shares in other countries must comply with the disclosure requirements of the 1933 Act, including the furnishing of a statutory prospectus, translated where necessary into the language of the persons to whom the offer is made. The SEC's rationale for the distinction is that mutual fund shares, unlike other securities, "are vigorously merchandised abroad to large numbers of small investors" and that "disclosure at the point of sale helps protect the U. S. securities market as a whole by insuring that foreign investors will not seek redemptions because of later realization that they had been inadequately informed about their investment. SA Rel. 5068 (1970). However, the SEC permits mutual funds to sell shares abroad at a sales load different from that applicable to U. S. sales where the fund can show that it is not economically feasible to sell abroad at the U. S. sales load and where the proposed sales load is not inconsistent with the laws of the country involved. Id.

Foreign Trading in U. S. Securities. Foreign persons who engage in transactions in securities of U. S. issuers may be subjected to liability under U. S. securities laws, provided the requisite use of the mails or facilities of interstate commerce is shown. A foreign mutual fund which owned more than 10% of the stock of a U. S. corporation has been held liable under SEA § 16(b) for profits realized from purchases and sales of its stock. Roth v. Fund of Funds, 405 F.2d 421 (2d Cir. 1968). The transactions in that case took place on a U. S. exchange, but the same result should be reached even if the transactions were effected abroad, since jurisdiction under § 16 results from the stock being registered under SEA § 12, rather than from use of interstate commerce facilities.

With respect to liability under SEA Rule 10b–5 for trading on inside information, one of the defendants in the landmark *Texas Gulf Sulphur* case was an engineer who lived in Canada and placed his order through a Toronto broker (he had, however, placed the order by telephone from New York and it was executed on a U. S. stock exchange). The court had no difficulty in finding the transaction subject to U. S. jurisdiction, nor in holding that the defendant could be validly served with process at his home in Canada. SEC

v. Texas Gulf Sulphur, 258 F.Supp. 262, 287 (S.
D.N.Y.1966) aff'd in part, rev'd in part, 401 F.
2d 833 (2d Cir. 1968).

Under SEA § 7, the Federal Reserve Board has
issued "margin regulations" limiting the amount
of credit that can be extended for the purchase
of U. S. securities (see § 24(a) *supra*). It is unclear whether these rules can be applied to foreign lenders who extend credit to U. S. purchasers of U. S. securities. See Metro-Goldwyn-May-
er v. Transamerica Corp., 303 F.Supp. 1354 (S.D.
N.Y.1969). However, in 1970, Congress amended
§ 7 to prohibit any "United States person" from
obtaining credit from a foreign lender in a transaction which would have been prohibited if it had
taken place in the U. S. Since that time, foreign
banks have been held subject to the margin regulations if they engage in transactions which can
be found to constitute doing business as a broker
or dealer in the U. S. U. S. v. Weisscredit, 325
F.Supp. 1384 (S.D.N.Y.1971); UFITEC v. Carter,
CCH ¶ 94,841 (Cal.Super.1974).

SEA § 13(d), which requires certain disclosures by any person or group which acquires
more than 5% of the stock of any company registered under SEA § 12, has been held applicable to
foreign investors, and the SEC has obtained injunctions against foreign investors and foreign
banks, requiring their compliance with the disclosure requirements. See SEC v. General Refracto-
ries, CCH ¶ 95,291 (D.D.C.1975).

§ 44. Foreign Transactions in Foreign Securities

There are a number of cases in which the courts have applied the antifraud provisions of the federal securities laws to transactions in foreign securities taking place outside the U. S. In some cases, the basis of jurisdiction has been the harm to U. S. shareholders of the corporation which was the alleged victim of the fraud. Schoenbaum v. Firstbrook, 405 F.2d 200 (2d Cir. 1968). In other cases, it has been based on the fact that some of the actions alleged to constitute the violation occurred within the U. S. Leasco v. Maxwell, 468 F.2d 1326 (2d Cir. 1972); Travis v. Anthes Imperial, 473 F.2d 515 (8th Cir. 1973).

In Bersch v. Drexel Firestone, 519 F.2d 974 (2d Cir. 1975), the court held that the antifraud provisions should be applied to:

(1) Sales to Americans residing in the U. S. whether or not any important acts occurred in the U. S.;

(2) Sale to Americans residing abroad if acts in the U. S. contributed significantly to their losses; and

(3) Sales to foreigners outside the U. S. only if acts in the U. S. caused their losses.

With respect to sales to foreigners, however, one court has already gone beyond this formulation, holding that "the federal securities laws * * * grant jurisdiction where at least some activity designed to further a fraudulent scheme occurs in this country, * * * We are reluctant to conclude that Congress intended to allow the United States to become a 'Barbary Coast,' as it were, harboring international securities 'pirates.' " SEC v. Kasser, 548 F.2d 109 (3d Cir. 1977); see IIT v. Vencap, 519 F.2d 1001, 1017 (2d Cir. 1975).

The validity of service of process outside the U. S. on a defendant in this type of action will depend on the extent of the defendant's activities in the U. S. Compare Alco Standard v. Benalal, CCH ¶ 93,640 (E.D.Pa.1972), and Rosen v. Dick, CCH ¶ 94,590 (S.D.N.Y.1974), with Bersch v. Drexel Firestone, 519 F.2d 974, 999 (2d Cir. 1975).

X. STATE REGULATION

The various federal securities laws specifically preserve the power of the states to regulate securities activities. See SA § 18; SEA § 28(a); ICA § 50; IAA § 222. Any transaction in securities, therefore, may be subject to the law of one or more states, in addition to federal law.

Every state has some law specifically regulating transactions in securities. These laws are known as "blue sky" laws, after an early judicial opinion describing their purpose as the prevention of "speculative schemes which have no more basis than so many feet of blue sky." Hall v. Geiger-Jones Co., 242 U.S. 539 (1917).

While these "blue sky" laws vary greatly from state to state, they generally contain the following three types of provisions (although not all contain all three types); (a) prohibitions against fraud in the sale of securities; (b) requirements for registration of brokers and dealers; and (c) requirements for registration of securities to be sold in the state.

In 1956, the Commissioners on Uniform State Laws promulgated a Uniform Securities Act (USA) for adoption by the states. Reflecting the pre-existing pattern of state laws and the differences in regulatory philosophy among the states, the act is divided into four parts; (1) antifraud provisions, (2) broker-dealer registration provisions, (3) security registration provisions, and (4) definitions, exemptions, and administrative and liability provisions. States are thus free to adopt one, two or all of the first three parts, plus the appropriate provisions of the fourth part.

While more than 30 states have adopted most or some of the provisions of the Uniform Act, the movement toward uniformity has been hampered by several factors. (a) Some of the most important commercial states, including New York, California, Illinois and Texas, have not adopted any part of the Act. (b) Almost all the states that have adopted it have made substantial changes from the approved text. (c) State administrators and courts interpret the same language differently, producing a difference in operation that is not apparent from a reading of the laws themselves.

Nevertheless, the promulgation and adoption of the Uniform Act has produced a much more rational and consistent pattern of regulation than previously existed. This development has also been assisted by the North American Securities Administrators (NASA), an association of state and provincial securities administrators, which from time to time issues "statements of policy" on various substantive and procedural questions and indicates to what extent those policies are followed by each of its members.

§ 45. Antifraud Provisions

In almost every state, the securities law contains some sort of general prohibition against fraud, and authorizes the appropriate government official to obtain injunctive relief or bring a criminal prosecution. The definition of fraud is usually worded in very general terms; the Uniform Act uses the language of SEC Rule 10b–5 (see § 18 *supra*) and makes it applicable to any "offer, sale, or purchase of any security." USA § 101.

§ 46. Broker-Dealer Registration

Almost every state requires securities broker-dealers and their agents to register with a state agency. Most of the statutes also contain provisions for denial or revocation of registration, or imposition of other sanctions. See USA § 204. The coverage of these provisions varies; some states define the term "broker-dealer" to include an issuer selling its own securities, but most do not. See USA § 401(c).

§ 47. Registration of Securities

With the exception of the New England and Middle Atlantic states, most of which have only rudimentary provisions for the registration of securities, almost every state requires that some affirmative action be taken to register securities before they can be sold in the state. This means that an underwriting syndicate making a national distribution of a new issue must take steps to "blue sky" the issue in more than 40 states in addition to complying with the federal Securities Act of 1933.

(a) Procedures

Most states which require registration of securities issues provide two alternative methods of registration: "notification" and "qualification." Some states provide a third method: registration by "coordination" for issues simultaneously being registered with the SEC.

Securities may generally be registered by "notification" only if they meet certain tests for stability and earnings coverage. See USA § 302(a). Registration is accomplished by filing a statement showing compliance with the statutory test, plus a description of the securities being registered and the terms of the offering.   USA § 302(b).   The registration automatically becomes effective within a prescribed period, unless the state administrator takes action to prevent it. See USA § 302(c).

Registration by "coordination" is substantially similar to registration by "notification" except that the only information normally required to be filed is a copy of the prospectus filed with the SEC under the 1933 Act.

Registration by "qualification" is the method generally prescribed for those issues which do not meet the tests prescribed for registration by other methods.   The issuer must file a statement containing information roughly comparable to that required in a 1933 Act registration statement, and registration does not become effective until the administrator takes action to approve it.

(b) Standards

In contrast to the 1933 Act, under which the SEC has no power to approve or disapprove the sale of securities, most state laws authorize the administrator to deny an application for registration, even though the facts regarding the security and the issuer are fully disclosed.   The standards for granting or denying an application range from those which authorize denial only on grounds of "fraud" to those which authorize the administrator to bar any issue unless he finds its terms to be "fair, just and equitable." Interpretations of these vague standards also vary greatly from state to state. The Uniform Act attempts to reduce administrative discretion in this area by authorizing denial of registration only if the administrator finds that the offering would tend "to work a fraud upon purchasers" or that it "would be made with unreasonable amounts of" underwriting compensation, promoter's profits, or options. USA § 306(a)(2)(E), (F). The associations of North American Securities Administrators and Midwest Securities Administrators have also issued a number of "Statements of Policy", indicating what levels of compensation or other arrangements with insiders would be considered unfair in determining whether registration of a particular issue should be granted.

(c) Exemptions

Most states exempt from their registration requirements the principal types of securities exempted from the 1933 Act—government securities, instruments issued by various types of institutions, and securities issued by companies subject to special regulatory statutes (such as banks and common carriers). In addition, most states exempt one important class of securities which are not exempt from the 1933 Act—namely, these listed on major stock exchanges. See USA § 402(a).

Private Placements. Traditionally, most state statutes did not contain exemptions comparable to the 1933 Act exemption for "transactions by an issuer not involving any public offering", although many had exemptions for "isolated transactions" or "pre-organization subscriptions." The Uniform Act established an exemption for offers "directed to not more than 10 persons," and recent state statutes or rules have tended to exempt offers or sales to less than a specified number of persons, in some cases following the tests laid down in SEC Rule 146 (see § 10(a) *supra*). The "sophistication" requirement in Rule 146 finds a counterpart in state provisions which commonly exempt any sales to broker-dealers, banks, or other financial institutions. See USA § 402(b)(8).

Interstate Offerings. The federal exemption for intrastate offerings in SA § 3(a)(11) finds a counterpart in provisions recently added to several state laws, notably those of New York and New Jersey, which exempt all offerings registered with the SEC and thus apply *only* to intrastate public offerings. See N.Y.Gen.Bus.Law § 359–ff; N.J.Stat.Ann. § 49:3–60. This exemption makes sense in the New York statute, which is basically a disclosure requirement; it makes less sense in the New Jersey statute, which authorizes the administrator to deny an application for registration on substantive grounds. See Data Access Systems v. State, 63 N.J. 158, 305 A.2d 427 (1973).

Secondary Transactions.   State securities laws do not embrace the "underwriter" concept of SA § 2(11), which has given rise to so much difficulty in determining when a person other than the issuer must register securities for sale under federal law (see § 10(e) *supra.*)   Most state laws have an exemption for "isolated non-issuer transactions" and for other non-issuer sales of securities listed on a major stock exchange or in "standard manuals" (such as Moody's and Standard & Poor's).   See USA § 402(b)(1), (2).   Under the Uniform Act, a registration of securities remains in effect for one year (unless suspended or revoked), and "all outstanding securities of the same class * * * are considered to be registered for the purpose of any non-issuer transaction" during that period.   USA § 305(i).

§ 48. Sanctions for Violations

Most state laws provide for a range of sanctions against persons who violate the registration or antifraud provisions.   The Uniform Act authorizes the administrator to conduct investigations, issue subpoenas and bring injunction actions, in addition to imposing criminal penalties for violations.   USA §§ 407–409.   The weak point of these provisions is that most states have a vey small staff engaged in administration and enforcement of their securities laws, so that as a practical matter the only significant sanction against violators is the threat of civil liability.

§ 49. Civil Liabilities

The traditional state securities law generally provides that any sale "made in violation of any provision" of the law is "voidable", and that the purchaser is entitled to rescind the transaction and recover his purchase price. The types of violations which give rise to this right of rescission may include many technical violations as well as a failure to register or a violation of the antifraud provisions. Thus, an issuer or broker-dealer making a public distribution runs the risk that a technical failure to comply with any provision of the securities law of a particular state will give all purchasers in that state an absolute right to the refund of their investment if the security declines in value. Enforceability is facilitated in many states by a requirement that issuers or broker-dealers post a surety bond for satisfaction of their liabilities.

The Uniform Act departs from the "voidability" concept to follow the approach of SA § 12. Any person who offers or sells a security (1) in violation of the registration requirements or certain other important provisions, or (2) by means of a misstatement or omission of a material fact, is made liable to refund the purchase price upon tender of the security, or to pay damages to the purchaser if he no longer owns it. USA § 410(a).

Persons Liable. Many state laws impose civil liability not only on the "seller", but also on any persons, or specified classes of persons, who "participate" or "aid" in the sale. The Uniform Act imposes liability on partners, officers and directors of the seller, whether or not they aid in the sale, and on other employees, broker-dealers and agents who "materially aid in the sale", subject in each case to a defense of "due diligence". USA § 410(b).

Implied Liability. In situations where the state law provides no express right of action to the purchaser in a transaction which violates the law, many courts have implied a right to rescind the transaction. The Uniform Act, however, contains a specific provision that it "does not create any cause of action not specified in" the Act. USA § 410(h). Since the Act creates no right of action for a violation of its general prohibition against fraud, this provision forecloses the development of implied rights of action for fraud which the federal courts have recognized under SEA Rule 10b–5 (see § 18 *supra*). This means that defrauded *sellers* of securities have no right of action under the Uniform Act. In one state which adopted the Uniform Act without § 410(h), the courts implied a private right of action on behalf of a defrauded seller. Shermer v. Baker, 2 Wash.App. 845, 472 P.2d 589 (1970).

§ 50.   Jurisdictional Questions

Most state securities laws apply to any offer or sale of securities in the state, but contain no explicit provisions defining when an offer or sale is made "in the state". Since many securities transactions involve a buyer in one state and a seller in another, difficult problems arise in determining (a) to which transactions the law of a particular state applies, and (b) which state law governs the validity of a transaction which has contacts with more than one state. For example, is an advertisement in a newspaper published in State A but also circulated in State B an "offer" in State B? If a broker in State A makes an offer by telephone to a customer in State B, who accepts the offer by mailing a check to the broker in State A, is the transaction voidable if the broker and the security were registered in State A but not in State B?

Applicable Law. Since most civil actions under the blue sky laws are in the nature of actions for rescission, courts traditionally tended to look to the conflict of laws principles applicable to contract claims, and to hold that the contract was not voidable if it was valid under the law of the state where the contract was made or to be performed. See, e. g., Robbins v. Pacific Eastern Corp., 8 Cal.2d 241, 65 P.2d 42 (1937). Under this approach, an issuer or broker-dealer could offer and sell securities to residents of a state with a "strict" blue sky law—without complying with the terms of that law—simply by making sure that the contract was technically made and performed in its own state. A more recent approach, however, is to hold that, when a customer is solicited in his home state, the securities law of that state must be complied with, no matter where the transaction is technically consummated. See Green v. Weis, Voisin, Cannon, Inc., 479 F.2d 462 (7th Cir. 1973). Where that approach is followed, the courts are also likely to hold that the law of the offeree's state cannot be avoided by providing in the contract that it shall be construed in accordance with the law of another state. Boehnen v. Walston & Co., 358 F.Supp. 537 (D.S.D.1973).

The Uniform Act adopts the latter approach by making the registration requirements applicable either when (1) an offer to sell is made in the state, or (2) an offer to buy is made and accepted in the state (since many offers take the form of the seller's solicitation of the purchaser's offer to buy). An offer to sell is deemed to be made in the state if it originates from the state, or is directed to and received in the state (except that advertisements in out-of-state newspapers or radio stations are not deemed to be made in the state.) An offer to buy is deemed to be accepted in the state when it is first communicated to the offeror in the state. USA § 414. Even this detailed specification can raise interpretive problems, however, particularly if the adopting state modifies the language of the Uniform Act.   See Kreis v. Mates Investment Fund, 473 F.2d 1308 (8th Cir. 1973).

Constitutional Questions.   In Merrick v. N. W. Halsey Co., 242 U.S. 568 (1917), the Supreme Court held, without discussion, that application of a state's blue sky laws to offers directed into the state by an out-of-state broker-dealer was not an unconstitutional interference with interstate commerce.   And in Travelers Health Ass'n v. Virginia, 339 U.S. 643 (1950), the Court held (5–4) that the Due Process Clause did not bar Virginia from issuing a cease and desist order under its blue sky law against a Nebraska association which solicited Virginia residents by mail and encouraged Virginia members to submit the names of their friends to the association's home office.

Personal Jurisdiction.   Under what circumstances can an issuer or broker-dealer which offers and sells securities to residents of a state be subject to suits in the courts of that state if it does not maintain any place of business there? Many state blue sky laws require an out-of-state applicant for registration to file a formal consent to service of process.   See USA § 414(g).   With respect to sales made without registration, in violation of state law, a number of states provide for "substituted" service of process.   Under these provisions, an out-of-state person who sells securities in the state in violation of its laws is deemed to have irrevocably appointed a named state official as his agent for service of process in any legal action or proceeding growing out of that conduct. See USA § 414(h); Paulos v. Best Securities, 260 Minn. 283, 109 N.W.2d 576 (1961). The constitutionality of these provisions, like other "long-arm" statutes, has been consistently upheld under the principles laid down by the Supreme Court in McGee v. International Life Ins. Co., 355 U.S. 220 (1957).

*

INDEX

INDEX
References are to Pages

[*294*]